A SUMMARY OF
THE NEW CATHOLIC CATECHISM

(Page ii is blank)

A SUMMARY OF THE NEW CATHOLIC CATECHISM

✠ JAMES A. GRIFFIN
Bishop of Columbus

ALBA·HOUSE   NEW·YORK

SOCIETY OF ST. PAUL, 2187 VICTORY BLVD., STATEN ISLAND, NEW YORK 10314

Library of Congress Cataloging-in-Publication Data

Griffin, James A.
     A summary of the new Catholic catechism / James A. Griffin.
          p.   cm.
     ISBN 0-8189-0714-2
     1. Catholic Church. Catechismus Ecclesiae Catholicae.
     2. Catholic Church — Catechisms — History and criticism. I. Title.
     BX1959.5.G75   1994
     238'.2 — dc20   94-28519
                                                        CIP

Produced and designed in the United States of America by the
Fathers and Brothers of the Society of St. Paul,
2187 Victory Boulevard, Staten Island, New York 10314,
as part of their communications apostolate.

ISBN: 0-8189-0714-2

National Library of Australia
Card Number and ISBN 1 875570 45 4

Printing Information:

Current Printing - first digit	1-	2	3	4	5	6	7	8	9	10

Year of Current Printing - first year shown

1994	1995	1996	1997	1998	1999

(Page iv)

Biblical Abbreviations

OLD TESTAMENT

Genesis	Gn	Nehemiah	Ne	Baruch	Ba
Exodus	Ex	Tobit	Tb	Ezekiel	Ezk
Leviticus	Lv	Judith	Jdt	Daniel	Dn
Numbers	Nb	Esther	Est	Hosea	Ho
Deuteronomy	Dt	1 Maccabees	1 M	Joel	Jl
Joshua	Jos	2 Maccabees	2 M	Amos	Am
Judges	Jg	Job	Jb	Obadiah	Ob
Ruth	Rt	Psalms	Ps	Jonah	Jon
1 Samuel	1 S	Proverbs	Pr	Micah	Mi
2 Samuel	2 S	Ecclesiastes	Ec	Nahum	Na
1 Kings	1 K	Song of Songs	Sg	Habakkuk	Hab
2 Kings	2 K	Wisdom	Ws	Zephaniah	Zp
1 Chronicles	1 Ch	Sirach	Si	Haggai	Hg
2 Chronicles	2 Ch	Isaiah	Is	Malachi	Ml
Ezra	Ezr	Jeremiah	Jr	Zechariah	Zc
		Lamentations	Lm		

NEW TESTAMENT

Matthew	Mt	Ephesians	Ep	Hebrews	Heb
Mark	Mk	Philippians	Ph	James	Jm
Luke	Lk	Colossians	Col	1 Peter	1 P
John	Jn	1 Thessalonians	1 Th	2 Peter	2 P
Acts	Ac	2 Thessalonians	2 Th	1 John	1 Jn
Romans	Rm	1 Timothy	1 Tm	2 John	2 Jn
1 Corinthians	1 Cor	2 Timothy	2 Tm	3 John	3 Jn
2 Corinthians	2 Cor	Titus	Tt	Jude	Jude
Galatians	Gal	Philemon	Phm	Revelation	Rv

Table of Contents

Book Two
The Celebration of the Christian Mystery

Book Three
Life in Christ

Book Four
Christian Prayer

(Page x is blank)

Introduction

The *Catechism of the Catholic Church* will certainly dominate the religious education which takes place in our schools, our religious education programs in our parish schools of religion, in the Rite of Christian Initiation of Adults (RCIA), and from the pulpits of our Church for decades to come.

Its publication flows from a request from the Synod of Bishops in 1985 for a comprehensive catechism of Catholic doctrine which would set forth in clear language the Church's teaching on faith and morals. The bishops asked that this compendium be biblical and liturgical in its foundations and adapted to the actual life of Christians. After extensive consultation with all of the bishops of the Church, the final text was approved by Pope John Paul II on June 25, 1992, and promulgated on December 8 of the same year.

The last truly international catechism for the Church came from the Council of Trent. It was known as the *Roman Catechism* and was published in 1566.

In our own country, the catechism of the Council of Trent was reflected in and replaced by the catechism of the Council of Baltimore (1885) and the many editions of this so-called *Baltimore Catechism* which followed the original. The *Baltimore Catechism* was the standard religious education instrument until the mid-1960's.

The *Catechism of the Catholic Church* is a great gift to us. It is an authentic and certain reference to Catholic faith and doctrine. It is a challenging document which can help us to reinvestigate and to reaffirm our faith as Catholics in our contemporary American culture.

The English text of the catechism runs some 700 pages. Cardinal Joseph Ratzinger, responding to questions at a conference on the *Catechism of the Catholic Church* in November 1993, spoke of the need for commentaries, summaries, and abridged editions of the catechism (cf. "Catechism Update," USCC, November 1993).

This present work is an attempt to respond to that need. I have endeavored to present a summary of the *Catechism of the Catholic Church* with special attention to the American Catholic culture in which we live and work out our salvation.

I express my thanks to all those who have assisted in the preparation of this text. Many have offered suggestions, corrections, criticisms, and encouragements to the original drafts which appeared as part of my weekly column in *The Catholic Times*, the newspaper of the Diocese of Columbus.

I express my special gratitude to my secretary, Mrs. Anita Rowe, who typed and retyped the various drafts of the text and assisted in the editing of the final copy.

(Page xiv is blank)

A SUMMARY OF
THE NEW CATHOLIC CATECHISM

Book One
The Profession of Faith

On October 11, 1992, the thirtieth anniversary of the opening of the Second Vatican Council, Pope John Paul II promulgated the *Catechism of the Catholic Church.*

This historic document "aims at presenting an organic synthesis of the foundations and essential contents of Catholic doctrine as regards both faith and morals, in the light of the Second Vatican Council and the whole of the Church's Tradition" (*Catechism of the Catholic Church*, No. 11).

Already several evaluations of this catechism have been offered. They range from seeing it as a unified and organized vision of the Catholic faith to viewing it as a tool to impose conservatism on the Church well into the third millennium of Christianity.

The catechism is addressed primarily to teachers of the faith, that is, bishops and educators, but its content and spirit will touch the life of every member of the Church. In these reflections, I hope to move through that catechism in an organized way, sharing its spirit and its content with you.

The outline of the catechism is traditional, centering around four bases: the baptismal profession of faith (Creed), the celebration of faith (Sacraments), the life of faith (Commandments), and the prayer of believers (the "Our Father").

The Human Capacity to Know God

The consideration of faith starts out by pointing out that the desire for God is written on the human heart. As St. Augustine put it so well, "Our hearts were made for you, O Lord, and they will never rest until they rest in you."

So it is natural for men and women to seek God and to develop friendship with him. But people can ignore, misunderstand, forget, or even positively reject this vital relationship with God.

The Church teaches that God's existence can be known with certainty from creation by the use of human reason alone. The traditional arguments in support of the existence of God are cited. From a consideration of movement, becoming, contingency, and the world's order and beauty, we can indeed reason to the existence of God.

We *can* reason to the existence of God, but we are not forced to do so. In fact, the conditions of life may well make it difficult or even impossible for many to follow this process. The concrete conditions of life restrict the time, or the opportunity, or the desire to pursue such a course. The consequences of sin also restrict this use of our intellectual ability. So God's revelation leads us to these truths which we could discover by our own unaided reason — and beyond.

The Communication of Revelation

The consideration of the story of God's revelation of himself starts from the premise that God had a definite plan to slowly reveal himself to mankind over the course of history. This revelation by God had as its final purpose or aim to enable all of us to know him and to respond to him in love and service in this world that we might enjoy eternal life with him forever in heaven.

God's self-revelation started with Adam and Eve. It survived original sin. It was solidified in the covenant with Noah after the flood. It was made even more specific in Abraham and in his calling to be the father of a multitude of nations. This self-revelation continued in the patriarchs, in Moses, in the prophets, and in the great men and women of the Old Testament.

Finally, in the fullness of time, God revealed himself in Jesus Christ, and in this full and complete revelation, he established the new covenant which will last until the end of time.

Revelation was completed with the Ascension of Jesus. As the catechism puts it so succinctly,

> "The Christian economy, therefore, since it is the new and definitive Covenant, will never pass away; and no new public revelation is to be expected before the glorious manifestation of Our Lord Jesus Christ" (*Catechism of the Catholic Church*, No. 66).

Yet, even if revelation is already complete, it remains for Christian faith gradually to explore and grasp more fully over the course of centuries its total significance and meaning.

God desires everyone to come to the knowledge of truth. To enable mankind to reach this goal, Christ commanded the apostles to preach the Gospel everywhere and to all people.

The apostles carried out this command, and they handed on the Gospel story both orally and in writing. To assure the preservation of this teaching and the continuation of this work, they left bishops as their successors, giving to them their own teaching authority.

This living communication of the Word of God is called "Tradition." It complements and completes the written communication of the Word of God, Sacred Scripture (the Bible).

> "Sacred Tradition and Sacred Scripture, then, are bound closely together, and communicate with one another. For both of them, flowing out of the same divine wellspring, come together in some fashion to form one thing and move towards the same goal" (*Dogmatic Constitution on Divine Revelation*, No. 9).

Thus, the Catholic Church has two sources of its truths, Sacred Scripture and Tradition. It accepts and reveres both of these sources of truth. They contain the deposit of faith, the core of our belief (*Depositum Fidei*).

To authentically interpret Scripture and Tradition is no easy task as witnessed to by the many controversies which have marked the history of Christianity. In the Catholic Church, this task is entrusted to the Magisterium of the Church, that is, the living teaching office of the pope and bishops.

> "The task of giving an authentic interpretation of the Word of God, whether in its written form or in the form of Tradition, has been entrusted exclusively to the living teaching office of the Church, whose authority in this matter is exercised in the name of Jesus Christ. Yet this Magisterium is not superior to the Word of God, but is its servant. It teaches only what has been handed on to it. At the divine command and with the help of the Holy Spirit, it listens to this devotedly, guards it with dedication, and expounds it faithfully. All that it proposes for belief as being divinely revealed is drawn from this single deposit of faith" (*Dogmatic Constitution on Divine Revelation*, No. 10).

The Church Magisterium proposes truths which are either contained in divine revelation or have a necessary connection with it as dogmas, that is, as truths to be accepted in faith by all Catholic people. Obviously, not all of these dogmas have an equal relationship to the basis of the Christian faith. Some are more closely connected than others. We acknowledge this variation when we speak of a "hierarchy of truth" in Catholic teaching.

Thus, in our faith, there is a threefold guarantee of truth, working together and guided by the Holy Spirit. These three forces are Sacred Scripture, Sacred Tradition, and the Magisterium of the Church. This "sense of faith" is also found among the people of God expressed in the daily prayer and action of their lives. As the Second Vatican Council expressed it,

> "By this appreciation of the faith, aroused and sustained by the Spirit of Truth, the People of God, guided by the Sacred Teaching Authority (Magisterium), and obeying it, receives not the mere word of men, but truly the word of God, the faith once for all delivered to the saints. The people unfailingly adheres to this faith, penetrates it more deeply with right judgments, and applies it more fully in daily life" (*Dogmatic Constitution on the Church*, No. 12).

The Scriptures: Our Heritage of Faith

In order to reveal himself to us more fully and more completely, God spoke to mankind in human words through the Sacred Scriptures.

The Church has always reverenced the Bible as the Word of God. In it, she finds nourishment and strength and support. She teaches that God himself is the author of Sacred Scripture. He used human instruments to accomplish his purpose, but these human instruments wrote what he intended and only what he intended.

> "To compose the sacred books, God chose certain men who, all the while he employed them in this task, made full use of their powers and faculties so that, though he acted in them and through them, it was as true authors that they consigned to writing whatever he wanted written, and no more" (*Dogmatic Constitution on Divine Revelation*, No. 11).

The Bible is very important to the Church, but our Church is not a "one source" Church. As we saw earlier, she looks to two sources of sacred truth, Scripture and Tradition. Misunderstanding of this position over the years has caused some to accuse the Church of not accepting the Scriptures, or not honoring the Scriptures, or not allowing its members to read the Scriptures.

Nothing could be further from the truth. The Church has been the preserver of the Scriptures. More — guided by Tradition which reaches back to the apostles themselves — the Church discerned which writings are to be included in the list of the sacred books of the Bible. Still more, the Church has led the effort to interpret the Scriptures from the very beginning.

Interpretation of the Scriptures is a serious and difficult science. To understand the author's message, the reader has to know the writer's background, the style of his/her writing, the times and culture of the setting of the book, as well as the intricacies of the original language or languages.

The search to understand the Bible is further complicated by the various senses that one can draw out of the Scriptures.

There is the literal sense, and there is the spiritual sense. This latter is further divided into allegorical, moral, and anagogical. The literal sense is the meaning conveyed by the words of Scripture and discovered by the science of exegesis, or "the drawing out of the meaning" through a linguistic and historical analysis of the text. The allegorical sense leads us to see the meaning of events by recognizing their oftentimes veiled significance in Christ. The moral sense leads us to act in accord with the justice and truth set forth in the Word of God. The anagogical sense leads us to see events in terms of their value in leading us toward heaven, our true homeland.

The Church reveres the 45 books of the Old Testament as the story of God's preparing the world for the coming of Christ. These books contain valuable truths about God, human life, and the mystery of our own eternal salvation.

The Church sees the four Gospels of the New Testament as "the" story of the life of Jesus and the beginnings of his Church. This story is amplified and developed in the Acts of the Apostles and the letters and writings which complete the 27 books of the New Testament.

These two Testaments, Old and New, form one unity. They are one because God's plan is one. They are one because God's revelation of himself and his Son is one. The story of the Bible then is a unified whole. The Old Testament is the period of preparation; the New Testament, the period of fulfillment. Knowledge of both of these Testaments leads us to better understand the entire story of salvation.

The Sacred Scriptures play a big part in the life of the Church. They form part of every liturgy. They weave their way through the administration of all of our sacraments. They are the heart of the public prayer of the Church, the Divine Office. They provide the basis for much of the prayer life and devotions of our present-day Church.

St. Jerome's words from the fourth century about the Scriptures apply with equal force today: "Ignorance of the Scriptures is ignorance of Christ."

God reveals himself to us in a variety of ways. His self-revelation is a call to us. This call is a call of love. His call seeks from each of us a personal response, the response of faith.

By faith we give ourselves completely to God and accept with our intellect and our will God's revelation. This acceptance is called "the obedience of faith." It is acceptance of God's Word simply because God, who is truth itself, guarantees its authenticity.

The Scriptures present to us an army of witnesses of faith, from Abraham, our spiritual father in faith, to Mary, the person who most perfectly achieved "the obedience of faith." The witness of their response to the call of faith serves as a model and an inspiration to each of us in our personal response.

Faith, then, is both a personal commitment to God and a free assent to the entire truth which God has revealed. This commitment and acceptance includes everything "contained in the Word of God, written or handed down, and ... proposed for belief by the Church as having been divinely revealed" (*Dei Filius*, No. 3).

Our Response to the Call: Faith

Faith is a gift from God. Without his giving us this gift, the act of faith is beyond us, but the act of faith is a truly human act. When God gives us the gift and we make an act of faith, placing our trust completely in him and accepting the truths which he has revealed because he has revealed them, we do not contradict human freedom or human reason. And to emphasize this point, God has given us many signs or "motives of credibility" which the human intelligence can grasp. Among these motives of credibility are the miracles performed by Jesus and the saints and the holiness and the growth of the Church.

12

Faith is certain. It gives us a certitude that surpasses all other human knowledge. It is founded on the truthfulness of God, who is truth itself.

Faith seeks understanding. Faith moves us to search out knowledge of the God in whom we have placed our faith. This deeper knowledge calls forth greater faith and the process goes on and on in an ever-deepening spiral of faith and knowledge, an ever-deepening acquisition of truth. This process is part of the wisdom which we acquire with age. The more we experience God, the better we know him; the better we know him, the deeper our faith grows.

Many try to set up a contradiction between faith and reason, but there can be no contradiction in truth. Truth is one. If there is a seeming contradiction, it is because we have not yet fully plumbed the depth of reason. As the Second Vatican Council said,

"Consequently, methodical research in all branches of knowledge, provided it is carried out in a truly scientific manner and in accord with moral norms, can never conflict with the faith, because the things of the world and the things of faith derive from the same God" (*Pastoral Constitution on the Church in the Modern World*, No. 36).

Faith in God is necessary for salvation. It is a gift which God extends to each of us. But this gift can be rejected, this gift can be lost. To persevere in faith we must strengthen it through prayer, reflection on

God's word, and a lifestyle which truly puts into practice what we believe.

Faith is a personal response to the call of God. But faith is not an isolated act. We live out our faith in a community, the community of the Church.

We express our faith in language taught to us by Mother Church. As our mother taught us the language of life, so the Church teaches us the language of faith. The language of the "formulas of faith" helps us to summarize what we believe, to celebrate our faith together in community, and to hand on our faith to others.

We express our faith in summaries or "professions of faith." These professions of faith are also called "Creeds" from the Latin word "credo" (I believe). The two creeds which are most familiar to us in the Church today are the Apostles' Creed, one of the basic prayers of faith, and the Nicene Creed, which we recite at most Sunday liturgies.

THE CREED

Let us walk together through the Apostles' Creed, taking a closer and more in-depth look at this formula of our faith.

I believe in God

This is the first and fundamental article of our faith. We believe in this one God who spoke to us through revelation and who was confirmed as Lord by Jesus and his Gospel.

God revealed himself progressively. The revelation of his name to Moses when he appeared to him in the midst of the burning bush is "the" most fundamental revelation. God told Moses that his name is "I Am Who Am" (Yahweh). Philosophers and theologians see in this name the roots of God's faithfulness, his unique "being," his truthfulness, and his love.

In the New Testament, God further reveals his nature to men through the doctrine of the Trinity. This Trinitarian belief is the foundation of the faith of every Christian. The Trinity is the central mystery of Christianity "because it is the mystery of God in himself and so the source of all other mysteries of faith, the light that enlightens them, and the most fundamental and essential dogma in the 'hierarchy of the truths of faith'" (*General Catechetical Directory*, No. 43).

God, the Father, is the source of the life of each of us. He is the authority figure in our lives. He looks on us with goodness and love. These are all activities we attribute to our natural father, so we call God "Father."

God, the Son, who became man and lived

among us is both our Savior and a model for our lives.

God, the Holy Spirit, is the wisdom of God, living within each one of us and guiding us to all truth.

The Trinity is and remains an absolute mystery, that is, even after God has revealed it to us, we cannot fully understand this truth. We believe because God who is truth has revealed it. Once it has been revealed, we can gain many insights into this mystery. We can see how it is not contradictory to human reason. We can see how fitting it is in the economy of salvation, but we will never fully understand the mystery of the Trinity.

There have been two approaches in the history of the Church to the understanding of the relationship of the three persons of the Trinity. Again, each gives valuable insight but neither exhausts the subject.

"The Eastern tradition emphasizes the Father's character as first source of the Spirit. By confessing the Spirit as 'coming from the Father,' it does not deny that he comes from the Father through the Son. The Western tradition stresses the communion 'of one being' between Father and Son, by saying, legitimately and with good reason, that the Spirit proceeds from the Father and the Son (filioque), for the eternal order of the divine persons in their communion of being implies that the Father, as the beginning without beginning, is the first source of the Spirit, but also that as Father of the only Son, the latter is, with him, 'the one principle from which the Holy Spirit proceeds' " (*Catechism of the Catholic Church*, No. 248).

We confess a oneness in the Trinity. We confess three distinct persons in the Trinity. We confess a uniqueness of relationship among the three persons of the Blessed Trinity, who remain of one nature or substance.

The Father Almighty

We believe that God is almighty, that is, he can do whatever he pleases with no effort or work on his part. Nothing is impossible for God.

Our belief in the power of God engenders a great sense of security within us. We know that God is our Father. We know he loves us. We know he can do whatever he pleases. Therefore, in whatever circumstances we find ourselves, we can always rely on his almighty power.

Evil and suffering, especially suffering of the innocent, seem to fly in the face of God's almighty power. We are confronted with the question of the existence of evil and suffering in our world constantly, and we ask "why?"

This is a difficult question to answer. Men and women have wrestled with it throughout recorded history. There is no simple answer. The example of

17

Jesus who suffered, though innocent, gives us some insight into this question. God brought good from what seemed to be the senseless suffering of his Son, and God brings good from the evil and suffering we experience in our world even though we do not often see how he does this. The whole of the Christian faith, the totality of Christ's message, is the only adequate answer to this vexing question of the existence of suffering and evil in our world.

Creator

Genesis, the first book of the Bible, begins "In the beginning when God created the heavens and the earth. . ." (Gn 1:1).

Creation is the fundamental act in God's plan. It is the beginning of history, all of which comes to a focus in one event, the coming of Christ. From that Christ-event flows out all of subsequent history. One can picture history as an hourglass in which all the sands of time move first toward a single focus, "the Christ-event," and then all subsequent movement of these same sands of time flow outward from the same focus or Christ-event.

Men and women have always wondered, speculated, and questioned the origins of our world and of the human race. Our age has made unprecedented progress toward answering those questions. Modern science is moving towards definitive answers about the "how" of our world. Faith goes beyond these questions of when and how our world began to answer the deeper question of the "meaning" of our origin, the "why" of life.

We are confident that human intelligence, unaided by faith, can come to an answer to those questions about our origin. More, human intelligence can reason to the fact of God's existence. But only through the gift of faith can that knowledge of God's existence be made certain, enlightened, and can our human response be clearly set forth. Through faith, we know clearly that God is the source and the goal of creation. We know that all creation is good. We know that men and women are called to a unique role in the stewardship of creation, and we know that sin has entered our world and that, through Christ, there is the sure hope of salvation for all of us.

Once God set his creation in order, he does not abandon it. He sustains us in life. He gives us the power to be ("In him we live, and move, and have our being," Ac 17:28) and he leads us to our final end or purpose in life.

God sustains and directs creation. But he does this in accord with the laws which he has set into motion at the time of creation. And he uses the cooperation of his creatures. The most wonderful of these cooperators is man himself. For God made us intelligent and free so that we might be his willing and able cooperators, perfecting creation and serving our neighbors' needs.

Human freedom is a startling proof of how much God does indeed love us. In the exercise of this human freedom, we reach our zenith, our fulfillment and perfection of being, but, alas, also in this exercise of human freedom we once more confront the existence and the problem of evil and suffering in our world.

Faith gives us the conviction that God would not permit any evil in our world without a good coming from it. We do not often see this good. How God brings good from the suffering and evil in our world is a question we shall not fully understand until we reach heaven. But faith assures us of the goodness of God and reminds us that God moves all creatures and all events toward goodness.

Of heaven and earth

God creates everything which exists. All creation is part of one unified whole created by God.

Purely spiritual beings, the angels, are part of God's creation. The existence of angels, spiritual, non-corporeal beings, is clear from both Scripture and Tradition. The word "angel" means "messenger." Indeed, that is the task we see angels fulfilling most often in the Scriptures. St. Augustine explains well:

"Angel" is the name of their office, not their nature. If you seek the name of their nature, it is "spirit"; if you seek the name of their office, it is "angel"; from what they are, "spirit," from what they do, "angel" (*En. in Ps.* 103, 15, 1).

Most of us became aware of the existence of angels through the teaching about our Guardian Angel, that is, a spirit assigned to us who stands by us always, seeking, in the words of the popular prayer, ". . . to light, to guard, to rule, to guide" (*Prayer to the Guardian Angels*). We are constantly reminded of the existence of angels, of their role in salvation, and of their role in our individual lives by the liturgy, the public prayer, and many popular devotions of our Church.

All of material creation comes from the hand of God as well. The crown of God's material creation is mankind, as only we are endowed with the gift of knowing and loving God in return. And, of natural creation, only we are destined to live forever in that love relationship with our Creator. We are a unity of body and soul. Our soul is created immediately by God. Our soul lives forever. The body is destined to die, but it is also destined to rise again in the final resurrection.

From the very beginning, God created man and woman in perfect equality as human persons. While each are complete in themselves, he created man and woman "for" the other and has willed their coming together as the first form of the communion

21

of persons and the source of the transmitting of human life.

From the Scriptures, we know that the first man and woman lived in an original state of justice, holiness, and perfection.

Genesis tells us in figurative language the story of our first parents' fall from innocence and the entrance of sin into our world.

The seriousness of sin can only be understood against the background of revelation.

> "Without the knowledge revelation gives us of God we cannot recognize sin clearly and are tempted to explain it as merely a developmental flaw, a psychological weakness, a mistake, or the necessary consequence of an inadequate social structure, etc." (*Catechism of the Catholic Church*, No. 387).

This explanation of sin clashes with our modern world's explaining or "explaining away" of the reality of sin. But revelation makes clear the entrance and the presence of sin in our world. It tells us how some of the angels, by an irrevocable choice, sinned and separated themselves from God forever. It tells us how our first parents, too, by their own free choice, sinned and separated themselves from God.

This first sin of Adam and Eve was a sin of disobedience. All of us, through the unity of the human race, are implicated in Adam's sin, and all of us receive a human nature deprived of its original holiness and justice. We call this deprivation "original sin." We describe ours as a "wounded" human nature, that is, a human nature not totally depraved but a human nature deprived of some of its original powers and thus subject to ignorance, suffering, sin, and death. We describe this inclination to sin as "concupiscence," and its presence in us makes our lives a constant struggle.

But God did not abandon us to our fallen condition. In the Book of Genesis (3:15), in what is called the "Protoevangelium" ("first or original Gospel"), he announced the coming of Jesus the Redeemer who would make up for the sin of the first Adam, as well as for the personal sins of each man and woman and open for all of us the way to victory over ignorance, suffering, sin, and death.

And in Jesus Christ, his only Son, Our Lord

In the fullness of time, St. Paul reminds us, God sent his Son to be our Redeemer (Gal 4:4-5).

His name is "Jesus," the name announced by the angel Gabriel when Mary consented to be his mother. "Jesus," which means "God saves," indicates both the divine origin of Jesus (God) and the divine mission of Jesus (redemption).

Another of his titles is "Christ." "Christ" comes from the Hebrew word for "anointed." Again, like the leaders of God's people before him, Jesus was chosen by the Father and anointed for his special mission, that of salvation.

"Son of God" is another title of Jesus. In the Old Testament this title was used to indicate a special relationship or intimacy which existed between God and one of his creatures. In the case of Jesus, this intimacy is even closer, the intimacy of oneness in the Trinity. Jesus is "more than human." At both the baptism of Jesus and at his Transfiguration, the Father gave vocal testimony of Jesus' sonship.

"Lord" is yet another of Jesus' titles. This is also drawn from the Old Testament where the word "Lord" was used in place of the inexpressible name for God, "Yahweh." This name clearly indicates the divinity of Jesus.

This Son, Lord, Savior, Anointed One, "Word of God" became flesh of the Virgin Mary, taking on our human nature in order to accomplish our salvation. We refer to this mystery of God becoming man as the "Incarnation."

Jesus is true God and true Man. Throughout history the Church has had to guard this truth against those who would either have Jesus' humanity assumed into his divinity, or his divinity reduced to the status of his being "the first among creatures." We believe Jesus is true God and true Man, two natures united in one person. Everything in Jesus' divinity is to be attributed to him; likewise, everything in Jesus' humanity is to be attributed to the same person, Jesus.

Our study of philosophy and of the meaning of the words "divine," "human," "nature," and "person," while not explaining away the mystery of the Incarnation, help us to see how this union, referred to as the "hypostatic union," is not a contradiction in terms.

The *Catechism of the Catholic Church* summarizes this duality of nature and oneness of person in these words:

> "Because 'human nature was assumed not absorbed,' in the mysterious union of the Incarnation, the Church was led over the course of centuries to confess the full reality of Christ's human soul, with its operations of intellect and will, and of his human body. In parallel fashion, she had to recall on each occasion that Christ's human nature belongs, as his own, to the divine person of the Son of God, who assumed it. Everything that Christ is and does in this nature derives from 'one of the Trinity.' The Son of God therefore communicates to his humanity his own personal mode of existence in the Trinity. In his soul as in his body, Christ thus expresses humanly the divine ways of the Trinity" (No. 470).

Conceived by the power of the Holy Spirit and born of the Virgin Mary

In God's eternal plan, prepared from all ages, his Son, Jesus, was to be conceived by the power of the Holy Spirit, the Lord and giver of life, and born of the Virgin Mary.

The prophet Isaiah promised this birth hundreds of years before the event in his words: "Look, the young woman is with child and shall bear a son" (Is 7:14). At the annunciation, the angel Gabriel announced to Mary that this child will be from the Holy Spirit: "The Holy Spirit will come upon you and the power of the Most High will overshadow you; therefore the child to be born will be holy; he will be called Son of God" (Lk 1:35). While Mary is carrying Jesus, her cousin Elizabeth hails her as "the mother of my Lord" (Lk 1:43).

Mary is outstanding among the servants of God, carefully awaiting the fullness of salvation. In anticipation of her unique role in this plan of salvation, Mary was preserved from all sin. Not only did Mary not commit any personal sin, she was, by the power of God, preserved from any stain of original sin. This belief of the Church, the dogma of the Immaculate Conception, was infallibly proclaimed by Pope Pius IX in 1854 in the decree "*Ineffabilis Deus.*"

> "The most blessed Virgin Mary was, from the first moment of her conception, by the singular grace and privilege of Almighty God and in view of the merits of Jesus Christ, the Savior of the human race, preserved immune from all stain of original sin."

The life of Jesus is traditionally divided into two parts, the hidden life and the public life of Jesus.

It is impossible to summarize the Gospels, "the story of the life of Jesus." The only way to know his life is to sit down, read and reflect on the accounts which Matthew, Mark, Luke, and John have left us. Every event of his life, from his birth to his Ascension, is for our teaching, our benefit. His words, his actions, his parables, his miracles, all meld together to give us the picture of his mission. Even those of us who have read this story hundreds of times receive new grace and new insight each time we pick up the Gospels and read part of the story of the life of Jesus.

Through its liturgical cycle of feasts, the Church helps us to live and relive this story of the life of Jesus, which is also the story of our redemption.

He suffered under Pontius Pilate,
was crucified, died . . .

The public life of Jesus came to its climax in the last week of his life. The Church relives these events each Holy Week. This part of the life of Jesus which details his passion, death and resurrection — referred to as "the Paschal Mystery" — is the very heart of the message which the followers of Christ and the members of his Church are to proclaim to the world.

The conflict between Jesus and the Jewish authorities came to a head during the Passover celebration in the third year of his public life. One can cite

27

many causes which contributed to this final confrontation. Religious leaders were jealous of Jesus' popularity with the people. His interpretation of the law "as one having authority" caused many to accuse him of not respecting the law and tradition of his people. His prediction of the destruction of the Temple in Jerusalem was distorted by many, including witnesses at his trial, to make Jesus seem to be an enemy of true religion and as one attempting to stir up rebellion against legitimate authority.

In reality, while all these reasons coalesced in the death of Jesus, the true cause of these final chapters of his life was his divine mission, our redemption. The personal guilt of the participants in Jesus' death is known to God alone. We cannot judge them. Still less can we lay responsibility for Jesus' death on the Jewish people of today. The Second Vatican Council spoke most clearly and forcefully on this matter.

> ". . . what happened in His passion cannot be blamed upon all the Jews then living, without distinction, nor upon the Jews of today" (*Declaration on the Relationship of the Church to Non-Christian Religions*, No. 4).

No, as the *Roman Catechism* teaches, "sinners themselves were the authors and, as it were, the instruments of all the pains that the divine redeemer endured" (*Roman Catechism* I, 5, 11).

Jesus died for our sins. That was the purpose of his coming into the world. That was the goal he set for himself and predicted to his apostles. That was the interpretation he himself gave to his death after his resurrection. His death was a freely chosen redemptive action.

And it is in this dying for our sins that Jesus demonstrates, beyond any shadow of a doubt, beyond even our capacity to understand, the unbelievable love which God has for each one of us.

"And it is by God's will that we have been sanctified through the offering of the body of Jesus Christ, once for all" (Heb 10:10).

It is this great sacrifice of love which we recall each time we partake in the Eucharist which Jesus instituted on the night before he died as an everlasting memorial of his sacrifice on the cross.

. . . and was buried

Jesus' being in the tomb established the connection between his life and his resurrection. It is the same Jesus, the same person who lived on earth, subject to all the limitations to which we are subject, sin alone excepted, who now lives glorious and immortal.

Through Baptism we are offered a share in that glorious life of the risen Jesus.

"Therefore we have been buried with him by baptism into death, so that, just as Christ was raised from the dead by the glory of the Father, so we too might walk in newness of life" (Rm 6:4).

He descended into hell

All of the just who had died before Jesus' death were awaiting the Redeemer to open the gates of heaven to them. They were in a state of deprivation of the vision of God, a state of "hell," as the Scripture terms it.

Jesus descended into this region to free the souls of the just who had preceded him in death. His conquest over sin and death was announced to them and made real and effective in their lives through this action on the part of Jesus.

On the third day he rose again

On the third day, Jesus rose from the dead. The empty tomb, the appearances of Jesus to his closest friends, to his disciples, to more than 500 people, come together to give a concrete proof of his resurrection. The mission and teaching of the apostles, as witnesses of the resurrection, are the foundation stones of the Church.

The resurrection of Jesus from the dead stands

at the very center of our Catholic faith. The Church vigorously resists the efforts of those who would attempt to give any other interpretation to this event. The stark reality is simply this: Jesus died; Jesus rose from the dead.

Jesus rose from the dead in a different state of being, a glorified state, a life which surpassed both the limits of our humanity and the limitations of death itself.

The resurrection of Jesus confirms all of his actions and teachings. It imparts "the" stamp of authority and authenticity on all that Jesus said and did during his life on earth.

The resurrection of Jesus is the fulfillment of the promises contained both in the Old Testament and in the teaching of Jesus himself. St. Paul alludes to this reality when he describes the resurrection of Jesus as being "in accordance with the Scriptures" (1 Cor 15:4).

The resurrection of Jesus is "the" proof of Jesus' divinity. By his own divine power, Jesus brought about his return to life: "I lay it down (my life) in order to take it up again. . . . I have the power to lay it down and I have power to take it up again" (Jn 10:18).

The resurrection of Jesus frees us from sin and opens for us the way to new life. This is the justification which Jesus came to share with us. This is our victory over sin and death. This is our opening to eternal life.

Jesus' resurrection is the foretaste and the promise of our own resurrection. His rising from the dead is the promise and source of our own resurrection. As St. Paul told the Corinthians,

"But in fact Christ has been raised from the dead, the first-fruits of those who have died . . . for as all die in Adam, so all will be made alive in Christ" (1 Cor 15:20-22).

*He ascended into heaven
and is seated at the right hand of the Father*

Christ's Ascension into heaven establishes the link between the one who descended from heaven in the Incarnation and the person, the God-man, who now enters heaven's domain. They are one and the same person. His Ascension also blazes the trail for all who will follow him into heaven. Where he has gone, we hope to follow. Finally, Christ's Ascension marks the beginning of the kingdom which will come to completion at the end of time.

He will come again to judge the living and the dead

With Christ's Ascension, God's plan has reached its final stages. Christ now reigns over his Church from his throne in heaven. The fulfillment of that kingdom over which he reigns is still ahead, destined to occur at a time unknown to us (cf. Ac 1:6-7). In the meantime, the Church, like Christ himself, must pass through many trials, sufferings, and persecutions, including a final and most troubling tribulation described in the Book of the Apocalypse. Following this period of test and trial, time will end, Jesus will come again in glory, and, as the Lord of life, he will judge and reward each human being.

I believe in the Holy Spirit

The Holy Spirit is the most difficult of the persons of the Blessed Trinity to comprehend. He is the first to come to us in order of grace, as his grace bestows the gift of faith. Without his activity within our souls, we are incapable of the initial act of faith. At the same time, the Holy Spirit is last to come in the revelation of the persons of the Holy Trinity. Knowledge of his existence follows knowledge of the Father and the Son. This same sequence was followed in revelation itself. St. Gregory Nazianzen says:

> "The Old Testament clearly proclaimed the Father, but the Son more obscurely. The New Testament revealed the Son and gave us a glimpse of the divinity of the Spirit. Now the Spirit dwells among us and grants us a clear vision of himself" (*Oratio Theol.*, 5, 26).

33

To help gain further insight into the person of the Holy Spirit, we might consider the names by which the Spirit is called and the symbols by which he is represented.

"Holy Spirit" is the name given to the third person of the Blessed Trinity by Jesus himself (Mt 28:19). He is the lifegiving breath of God. He is called the "Paraclete" because he is our advocate with the Father. He is called "Spirit of Truth" as he is the source of all truth and reveals all truth through the disciples of Jesus, reminding them of "everything" which Jesus taught.

The images of the Spirit include water (a sign of new life), fire (transforming energy), cloud and light (a glory, sometimes veiled, sometimes re-vealed), a seal (an indelible impression on the soul). Each of these images gives us new insight into the role of this third person of the Blessed Trinity.

This Spirit has been active from the beginning of creation in the story of God's dealing with his children. He is hovering over the void as the story of Genesis begins. He is present and active in creation, in the promise of redemption, and in the great theophanies of the Old Testament. We find him in the critical moments of the history of God's chosen people, in the many predictions of the coming of the Messiah, and in the immediate preparation for Jesus' birth. He is active in the preparation for the public life of Christ in his life, death, and resurrection, and in the establishment of his Church at Pentecost. He continues his lifegiving role throughout history.

Even today, he continues to build, anoint, and sanctify the Church.

We now turn our attention to a consideration of the Church which Jesus established.

I believe in the Holy Catholic Church

Our belief in the Church flows from our core belief in the Trinity. We believe "in" the Church in a different sense than we believe "in" God the Father. The one belief flows from the other, and belief in the Church could not exist without that foundational act of faith in God. The Church depends entirely on the Father.

Likewise, the Church depends entirely on the Son. As the early Fathers of the Church put it, the Church is like the moon. It shines, but only because it reflects the light of the sun, which is its source of light. This sun, of course, is Jesus himself.

In equal measure, the Church depends on the Holy Spirit. It is the Spirit who gives holiness and life and vitality to the Church.

The Church is a gathering of people for a religious purpose. The *Catechism of the Catholic Church* defines the Church as "the assembly of those whom God's Word 'convokes,' i.e., gathers together to form the People of God and who themselves, nour-ished with the Body of Christ, become the Body of Christ" (No. 777). In this sense of the word, we apply the term to the liturgical assembly of believers, to the local community of believers, and to the universal community of believers.

There are many images, figures, and symbols applied to the Church. In the Old Testament, the chief image is that of the People of God. In the New Testament, the chief image for the Church is the Body of Christ. Around these two central images, a virtual lexicon of images, symbols, and figures have been assembled, each pointing out or giving insight into some facet of this mystery which we call "Church."

This "gathering" of the People of God into Church was part of God's plan from the very begin-ning. The "gathering" began, in point of fact, at the moment of our first parents' sin. This sin separated humans from their God and made a new gathering necessary. Throughout the course of God's dealing with his people in the Old Testament, the gathering continued, all pointing towards the coming of Christ and his immediate work in the establishment of his Church. This "gathering" continues today in an ever-widening missionary embrace which will reach its perfection in the kingdom of heaven.

The Church came into existence through the total sacrifice of Jesus, anticipated in his establishment of the sacrament of the Holy Eucharist and brought to culmination by his death on the cross. From this sacrifice and from the consequent gift of the Holy Spirit to the apostles on that first Pentecost, the Church was born.

The Church is a combination of both human and divine elements, a mystery which both is part of human history and, yet, at the same time, something which transcends human history. As the *Catechism of the Catholic Church* describes it, she is,

> "a society structured with hierarchical organs and the Mystical Body of Christ;
> the visible society and the spiritual community;
> the earthly Church and the Church endowed with heavenly riches" (No. 771).

This Church is a sacrament, a sacred sign, an instrumental and effective sign of our unity with God and our unity with one another.

The Church, the People of God

The image of the Church as the People of God received new impetus from the Second Vatican Council's *Dogmatic Constitution on the Church* and has been prominent in discussions on the Church in the decades after the Council.

The People of God is a unique grouping. It is a people gathered from disunity into one by God's calling them by name. Membership in the People of God comes through the sacrament of Baptism. This membership makes a man or woman part of the Body whose head is Christ. It establishes him or her in the condition of the freedom of a child of God, able to live in accord with the great commandment of love which Jesus left us. Membership commits one to the mission of being "a light to the world" and promises the destiny of eternal life in the kingdom of heaven. In the unity of this one people, there is a great diversity of members, of functions, of gifts and charisms. As different and distinct as each member is, all are joined to one another, especially to the poor, the persecuted, and the marginalized of this world.

How does one come to recognize the Church of Christ? In the Creed, we profess her four distinguishing characteristics: one, holy, catholic, apostolic.

The Church is one. She is one in her Source, one in her Founder, one in her soul or spirit, one in her faith, one in her worship, and one in her apostolic succession. The same *Dogmatic Constitution on the Church* tells us:

> "This Church, constituted and organized as a society in this present world, subsists in the Catholic Church, which is governed by the

successor of Peter and by the bishops in communion with him . . ." (No. 8).

Despite the wounds to unity inflicted by men and women throughout history, the Church is one and presses always towards greater unity.

The Church is holy. Jesus himself is her Founder and gives the Church the gift of holiness. The Holy Spirit abides in her and is her soul of life, engendering holiness in her members. Her members are indeed holy. In Mary, the mother of Jesus, we have the perfect example of the holiness of the Church. Other members have been "canonized," that is, solemnly proclaimed after their death to have been saints, men and women who lived exemplary holy lives. And all members are to strive for holiness. Striving for holiness is part of the essence of the Church. Again, the *Dogmatic Constitution on the Church* says:

> "Christ, 'holy, innocent, undefiled' (Heb 7:26), knew nothing of sin (2 Cor 5:21), but came only to expiate the sins of the people (cf. Heb 2:17). The Church, however, clasping sinners to her bosom, at once holy and always in need of purification, incessantly pursues the path of penance and renewal" (No. 8).

The Church is catholic. "Catholic" means "universal, possessing the characteristics of totality or wholeness." The Church is universal because Christ is present in her in his fullness. Wherever the Church is, Christ is present. The Church is catholic in another sense as well. Her mission is total, universal. She is called to bring the good news of the Gospel to every person, to every nation, to every corner of the world.

This catholicity of the Church exists in each particular or local church as well as in the universal Church. Each individual church with the universal Church has both the mandate and the mission to preach the Good News. By her very nature, the Church is missionary. The Holy Spirit leads the Church along this missionary path. And to this Church, all men and women stand in some relationship, even if they are completely unaware of that bond.

The *Dogmatic Constitution on the Church*, in a beautiful passage well worth reading and reflecting on (Nos. 14, 15 and 16), explores this wondrous relationship.

The Church is apostolic. She is apostolic because she is founded on the apostles. She is apostolic because, guided by the indwelling of the Holy Spirit, she teaches the truths of faith learned from the apostles. She is apostolic in that she continues to be taught, guided, and made holy by the successors of the apostles, the college of bishops in union with the successor of Peter, the Holy Father.

This one, holy, catholic, and apostolic Church

40

will endure until the end of time (the gift of indefectibility). She will preserve the truths of Christ (the gift of infallibility) until the end of time.

Christ's Faithful: Priests and Laity

By Baptism, all Christians receive an equality of dignity and action, but the Lord has willed a diversity in ministry among them.

Christ himself is the source of ministry in the Church. He is the source of its existence, of its authority, of its mission, of its orientation, and of its goal.

The sacramental ministry to act in the person of Christ in the Church is conferred by a special sacrament (Holy Orders). This call to ministry is a personal call to collegial service of one's brothers and sisters. Individual bishops are the source and principle of unity in their churches. They are gathered together in geographic groupings (provinces or regions), in national or international groups (episcopal conferences), and gathered "in toto" as the college of bishops. This college of bishops, through ecumenical councils and in union with the Pope, exercise power over the entire Church. The Pope himself stands as both the sign and cause of the unity of the bishops and of the entire community of the faithful.

Through sacramental ordinations, bishops and priests share in the threefold office of Jesus: teaching, governing, sanctifying.

The first task of the bishop, with the priests as his co-workers, is to proclaim the Gospel. The Magisterium or teaching voice of the Church guarantees the integrity of this teaching office. We talk about the extraordinary and the ordinary Magisterium of the Church. Really, they are one. The difference is the explicitness of the presence of the Holy Spirit's guidance. The *Catechism* succinctly explains these two aspects of the Magisterium:

> "'The Roman Pontiff, head of the college of bishops, enjoys this infallibility in virtue of his office, when, as supreme pastor and teacher of all the faithful who confirms his brethren in the faith he proclaims by a definitive act a doctrine pertaining to faith or morals.... The infallibility promised to the Church is also present in the body of bishops when, together with Peter's successor, they exercise the supreme Magisterium,' above all in an Ecumenical Council. When the Church through its supreme Magisterium proposes a doctrine 'for belief as being divinely revealed,' and as the teaching of Christ, the definitions 'must be adhered to with the obedience of faith.' This infallibility extends as far as the deposit of divine Revelation itself.
> Divine assistance is also given to the successors of the apostles, teaching in communion with

the successor of Peter, and, in a particular way, to the Bishop of Rome, pastor of the whole Church, when, without arriving at an infallible definition and without pronouncing in a 'definitive manner,' they propose in the exercise of the ordinary Magisterium a teaching that leads to better understanding of revelation in matters of faith and morals. To this ordinary teaching the faithful 'are to adhere to it with religious assent' which, though distinct from the assent of faith, is nonetheless an extension of it" (Nos. 891-892).

The bishop and his priests share Christ's sanctifying office. They accomplish this office by their prayer, work, ministry of word and sacrament, especially the Eucharist, and by the example of their own lives.

Finally, the bishop and his priests share Christ's ruling office. The bishop governs the local church with a power which is proper, ordinary, and immediate. He also, in communion with all the bishops under the leadership of the Pope, contributes to the governance of the entire Church.

The lay members of the Church through Baptism also share, each in accord with his or her own vocation, the priestly, prophetic, and kingly mission of Christ. All work together to proclaim and bring about the establishment of Christ's kingdom.

I believe in the communion of saints

The Church is communion of holy things (de-rived from the merits of Christ) and of holy persons (people who have reached or are striving towards holiness of life).

These "holy persons" include the pilgrim people on earth, those who have died and are in the process of purification, and those who have attained heaven and live in the glory of God. These latter help their sisters and brothers by their own holiness, which strengthens the entire communion of saints, and by the example of their lives on earth. The souls in purgatory are the object of prayer by the pilgrim people on earth. The prayers of the living members of the Church assist these souls on the last stage of their journey and move them, in turn, to be effective intercessors for their sisters and brothers on earth when they reach heaven.

Mary

It is natural that, after speaking of the Church and its story, we turn to consider Mary, who is the "Mother of the Church" (Paul VI, *Discourse*, 21 November 1964) and the most perfect example of the disciple of Christ. Mary is the preeminent member of the Church.

Mary's role flows from Christ and is inseparable from him. It is because of this close and perfect cooperation with her Son that she is given titles such as "Mother of the Church," "Cause of Our Joy," "Queen of the Apostles," "Help of Christians." Among the early Greek fathers, she was given the preeminent title of *"Theotokos"* (God bearer) indicating that it is from her divine maternity that all of her other privileges and titles flow. In this context of relationship to the Church, we might coin a word and call her *"Ecclesiatokos"* (bearer of the Church).

Because of her perfect cooperation with God in the plan of redemption, Mary was preserved from all stain of sin, even original sin, from the first moment of her existence (the Immaculate Conception). Throughout her life, she was "full of grace." And as the crowning glory of her existence on earth, she was assumed, body and soul, into heaven (the Assumption). This truth about Our Lady was infallibly defined by Pope Pius XII in 1950:

> "And finally the Immaculate Virgin, preserved from every stain of original sin, when the course of her earthly life was finished, was taken up body and soul into the glory of heaven, and exalted by the Lord as Queen of all, so that she might be more fully conformed to her Son, the Lord of Lords and conqueror of sin and death" (*Munificentissimus Deus*, 1950).

In heaven, Mary already shares fully in the glory of the resurrection. From her place in heaven, she continues by her prayers to intercede for us. All of her efforts, as our Mother, flow from the super-abundance of the merits of her Son.

It is only natural that great devotion to Mary has developed over the years. This has been a source of great joy and grace to many. Sadly, devotion to Mary has been misunderstood, at times, by both those inside and outside the Church. This misunder-standing has led to a misperception by those outside the Church of our stance before Mary. We venerate her as the greatest of saints. We do not worship her or place her on equal footing with her Son. Within the Church, misunderstanding of Mary's role has led, at times, to gross understatements or overstate-ments of her role in salvation history.

As the "new Eve," Mary continues to be Mother of the Church and Mother to each one of her sons and daughters.

I believe in the forgiveness of sins . . .

Associated with both the Holy Spirit and the communion of saints is the forgiveness of sins. It is the Spirit who forgives sins, and it is through mem-bership in the communion of saints that one's faith opens the possibility to the two great sacraments of forgiveness of sins: Baptism, full and complete re-mission of original sin and any actual sins, and Reconciliation, the "second plank after shipwreck."

The resurrection of the body . . .

We believe not only that our souls will live on after death, but that our mortal bodies will also come to life again. Although much opposed in the course of history, our belief in the resurrection of the body is linked to belief in Jesus himself and is most clear. What do we believe? We believe that our mortal body shall rise. Who shall rise? All the dead shall rise. When will this take place? The resurrection of the body will take place at the end of time. And how will it take place? This is beyond our understanding, even our imagination. We accept the resurrection of the body through faith in Jesus who said, "I am the resurrection and the life" (Jn 11:25).

For us then, death takes on a whole new meaning, a positive meaning. Death remains a consequence of sin. Death remains the end of earthly life. But Christ, by his own death and resurrection, has transformed death. As the Preface of the funeral liturgy sings,

> "Lord, for your faithful people, life is changed, not ended. When the body of our earthly dwelling lies in death, we gain an everlasting dwelling-place in heaven" (*Preface of the Dead*, No. 1).

And life everlasting

Death, then, is another step on the continuum of life for us. We believe that immediately after death we are each judged and rewarded in accord with our faith and our good work.

There are three possible outcomes of this immediate or particular judgment. Those who die in God's grace and friendship, purified from all sin and punishment due for sin, enter into heaven where they live forever in perfect happiness with God in an existence beyond our capacity to even imagine.

"No eye has seen, nor ear heard, nor the human heart conceived, what God has prepared for those who love him" (1 Cor 2:9).

Those who die in God's friendship but not perfectly purified from sin and the effects of sin undergo a process of purification after death in purgatory and then enter the presence of God. Our teaching on purgatory is supported by both Scripture and by the constant tradition of the Church in its practice of prayer for the dead. Finally, those who do not die in God's grace, who by their own free decision have excluded themselves from his friendship, are forever separated from him. This separation is the chief punishment of the state of hell.

Besides this particular judgment, we look forward to a general judgment at the end of time when

Jesus will return in glory. The certainty of this last judgment summons us to conversion while we have time, inspires in us a holy fear of God, and impels us to work for the justice of his kingdom, inspired by a blessed hope of reward at the time of his return.

It is in this final return of Jesus as judge that the kingdom of God will be established in its fullness and the "new heavens and new earth" (Rv 21:1) will be forever established.

This completes our review of the first book of the *Catechism of the Catholic Church*.

Book Two
The Celebration of
the Christian Mystery

The Liturgy

The *Catechism of the Catholic Church* turns
from the Creed to a consideration of the celebration
of the mystery of Christ in the liturgy.

"Liturgy" means "work of the people." It is both a
work of the people and for the people. In the
liturgy, the mystery of Christ is proclaimed so that
all the people can live that mystery to its fullest
and proclaim by their words and actions that same
mystery to the entire world. The liturgy is the
action of the Church, the prayer in which all
Christian prayer finds its source and its summit.

Catechesis has a direct relationship with liturgy.
It is the task of catechesis to make clear Christ's
action in all of its fullness in the sacraments,
effecting the transformation of the human
being. This special end or aim of catechesis is
given the name "mystagogy."

Let us now look at the liturgy of the Church.
In this explanation of the sacraments, we will talk
first of the sacramental economy, then we
will look at the sacramental celebration. Finally,
we will look at the seven special encounters
with the Lord Jesus and his saving activities
which we name "sacraments."

The bestowal of the Holy Spirit upon the apostles at Pentecost began a new era in God's relationship with his people, the Age of the Church. During this time, Christ shares his gift of salvation through the liturgy of his Church. We call this special action of sharing salvation "the sacramental economy." This economy, or process, will be in force until the end of time when Christ comes again in glory.

This is a new chapter in a continuing story. From the very beginning of time, salvation is a unified, divine blessing, but it has different chapters. From creation, God blessed all his creatures and pronounced them "good." In his relationship with his chosen people, his extraordinary interventions into their history are manifestations of this same special blessing. In the Church's life and in her liturgy, the same goodness and blessing is both revealed and communicated. The liturgy acknowledges this blessing and at the same moment implores the continued bestowal of the same blessing on all of God's creation.

The paschal mystery is a unique event. While it occurred at a moment of history and can be located in that moment, it cannot be "fixed" in that moment of the past. Through the apostles and their successors, Christ continues his work of salvation. He continues it through the sacraments, outward signs consisting of words and actions which both signify grace and at one and the same time make real and effective in the lives of the recipients the grace which they signify.

The liturgy is an encounter with Christ, but it is also the work of the Trinity. It is the gift of the Father, and it is the work of the Spirit.

Assisted by the work of the Spirit, the liturgy helps us understand the Word of God in the Scriptures. Likewise, the Spirit is involved in each sacramental celebration, especially in the Eucharist. He is invoked in the *epiclesis* wherein the Father is asked to send the special gift of the Son through the work of the Spirit. The Spirit's work is also memorialized in each celebration in the *anamnesis*.

In every liturgy, it is the Spirit who brings us together as a body. It is the Spirit who brings us into union with Christ and his saving activity.

The Paschal Mystery in the Church's Sacraments

It is clear from what we have seen that the whole liturgical life of the Church centers around the eucharistic sacrifice and the sacraments. The seven sacraments of the Church are: Baptism, Confirmation, Eucharist, Reconciliation, Anointing of the Sick, Holy Orders, and Matrimony.

These seven encounters with Christ have several common elements, both from a doctrinal point of view and in the manner of their celebration.

From the doctrinal point of view, the seven sacraments are all instituted by Christ. Through the guidance of the Holy Spirit, they have all been recognized by the Church as special encounters with him. Likewise, the determination of how they are administered is entrusted to the Church, again under the guidance of the Holy Spirit. More, they are dispensed by the Church through the mission or work of the Holy Spirit. They, likewise, are "for the Church" as they build up the body of the Church.

The seven sacraments have a common purpose which is to make people holy. They sanctify the individual; they contribute to the building up in holiness of the community of the Church.

The sacraments are all effective. They accomplish or bring about what the words and actions signify. By the very fact that the action of the sacrament is placed, independent of the merits of the celebrant or recipient, the sacrament is rendered present (*ex opere operato*). This is because any sacrament derives its power from the saving merits of Jesus Christ.

We are not saying that the merits of the celebrant or recipient do not enter into the reception of the sacrament. The existence of the sacrament does not depend on them, but the fruits of the sacrament are indeed conditioned on the merits of the one who accepts or receives the sacrament (*ex opere operantis*).

The fruits of the sacrament affect both the

individual and the body of the Church. The individual grows in love, the entire body of the Church grows in life in Christ Jesus.

We now turn our attention to the celebration of the seven sacraments. Again, we will start by describing elements common to their celebration, then we will look at each of the sacraments individually.

A consideration of the common elements of the celebration of the sacraments will answer the questions: Who celebrates? How do we celebrate? When do we celebrate? Where do we celebrate?

Who celebrates? The entire Church celebrates every sacrament. This explains why liturgical services are never private functions. It also explains why an individual or group cannot take it upon itself to change the administration of a sacrament. Every sacrament is the work of the Church; each member functions in accord with his or her special call in the celebration of the sacraments.

How do we celebrate? We celebrate with signs and symbols. These are signs and symbols of our human world, signs and symbols of the covenant of God with his chosen people. These are signs and symbols which have been taken by Christ and transformed into sacramental signs. He gave these signs and symbols a new meaning which brings about an encounter with the Father, through the Son, in the power of the Holy Spirit. As the *Catechism* puts it:

"The liturgical celebration involves signs and symbols relating to creation (candles, water, fire), human life (washing, anointing, breaking bread) and the history of salvation (the rites of the Passover). Integrated into the world of faith and taken up by the power of the Holy Spirit, these cosmic elements, human rituals, and gestures of remembrance of God become bearers of the saving and sanctifying action of Christ" (No. 1189).

When do we celebrate? We celebrate each Sunday in a special way as this is the day on which we keep the memory of the resurrection of the Lord. Easter is the center of this celebration, the heart of our liturgical year.

Through the cycle of the year, we recall the principal events of Jesus' life, those which led up to and prepared for the events of the Easter Triduum, as well as those flowing out of the Easter Triduum as the firstfruits of his work of redemption.

Parallel to this cycle we have a second series of celebrations commemorating the role of Mary, the Mother of God, in redemption and presenting the great heroes and heroines of life in Christ, the saints. We call this cycle of saints the "sanctoral cycle."

Where do we celebrate? We celebrate wherever the living Body of Christ is assembled. Whenever possible, we construct houses of worship in which to hold these celebrations. These churches are our gathering places. They are also signs of the

Church living in the midst of this world. Finally, they stand as witnesses to the age to come when Jesus will come again in glory at the end of time.

We begin our consideration of the individual sacraments with the sacraments of initiation: Baptism, Confirmation, and Holy Eucharist. These are the sacraments which fully incorporate a person into the Church and lay the foundation of the Christian life.

Baptism

Baptism is the basic building block of the Christian life. To "baptize" means to plunge or immerse. In Baptism, we are plunged into water to symbolize our dying with Christ from which we rise as a new creation. Being plunged into water also signifies a cleansing, a cleansing from all sin which is effected by our association with the death and resurrection of Jesus Christ.

Baptism is clearly prefigured in many places in the Old Testament. In the Easter Vigil ceremony, we recall some of these prefigurements: the waters at the very beginning of creation over which the Spirit of God hovered, the waters of the great flood, the waters of the Red Sea, the waters of the Jordan River.

After his resurrection, Jesus gave his apostles the command to baptize.

"Go, therefore, and make disciples of all nations, baptizing them in the name of the Father,
and of the Son, and of the Holy Spirit, and
teaching them to obey everything that I have
commanded you" (Mt 28:19-20).

The Church has celebrated Baptism from the
day of Pentecost, the beginning of the Church, to the
present. Always, it has been accomplished in stages.
Presently, in the Baptism of infants, these steps or
stages are encapsulated into a single ceremony, but
they are still clearly distinguishable. In the Baptism
of adults presently, the rite is normally divided into
several distinct and separate stages found in the Rite
of Christian Initiation of Adults (RCIA). Always, the
essential elements remain the same and central to
the ceremony.

Baptism is accomplished by immersion or by
the pouring of water on the forehead of the candidate while pronouncing the words "I baptize you in
the name of the Father, and of the Son, and of the
Holy Spirit."

In the solemn administration of Baptism, the
act of baptizing is followed by an anointing with
chrism to signify the gift of the Holy Spirit, by the
presentation of a white garment to signify that the
baptized is now "clothed in Christ," and by the
presentation of a lighted candle to signify that the
person has now been "enlightened" in Christ and
called to become "a light to the world."

Children are baptized with reliance on the parents and sponsors to assist the unfolding of the grace of Baptism in their lives. Adults usually go through a period of preparation for Baptism (the catechumenate) and a follow-up to Baptism (the *mystagogia*) to equip them to assist in the unfolding of the graces of Baptism in their own lives.

The normal minister of Baptism is the bishop, priest, or deacon. In cases of necessity, however, anyone can baptize if he or she intends to do what the Church does in Baptism and uses water and the Trinitarian formula recited above.

Baptism is necessary for salvation. Those who have heard the Gospel and have opportunity to receive the sacrament must receive it. If one suffers death for and with Christ, the Church recognizes this as a baptism of blood. For those who desire Baptism but do not have the opportunity to receive it, the Church recognizes a baptism of desire. To summarize the Church's teaching on the necessity of Baptism: "God has bound salvation to the sacrament of Baptism, but he himself is not bound by his sacraments" (*Catechism of the Catholic Church*, No. 1257).

Baptism forgives all sin, both original and actual. It bestows an everlasting mark or character of belonging to Christ on the soul of the one baptized. It bestows the theological gifts of faith, hope, and charity. It makes one a member of the Church, the

Body of Christ. It gives a share in the common priesthood of all the believers.

Confirmation

Confirmation, the second of the sacraments of Christian initiation, is necessary for baptismal grace to have its full effect in the life of the Christian. From the time of the apostles, this gift of the Spirit has been given to the baptized. Its roots run deep into the Old Testament and its many prophecies about the presence of the Spirit of the Lord with his people and especially with the expected Messiah. This presence of the Spirit was manifested in a special way at Pentecost and was declared by St. Peter in his first sermon (Ac 2:14-21) to be a sign of the messianic age.

Confirmation is bestowed through the laying on of hands and, from earliest years in the Church, an accompanying anointing with perfumed oil. This chrism is specially blessed by the bishop each year at a special liturgy, usually on or near Holy Thursday.

Anointing with oil has a long and rich history in the story of God's people. It signifies abundance in joy; it cleanses and limbers; it heals; it makes radiant with beauty, health and strength.

Through this anointing, the recipient of the sacrament of Confirmation receives the seal of the Holy Spirit. This seal marks the recipient as belonging to Christ and as being a servant of Christ. Likewise, the seal of Confirmation marks the recipient as one who is promised the special protection and assistance of God.

The present rite of conferring the sacrament of Confirmation retains the prayer over the candidates with extended hands, the anointing with chrism, and the formula: "N, be sealed with the gift of the Holy Spirit."

Like Baptism, Confirmation imprints an indelible, spiritual mark or character on the soul. It bestows a new outpouring of the Holy Spirit. It increases and deepens baptismal grace. It imparts the seven gifts of the Holy Spirit which stay with the recipient and work in him or her for a lifetime. Finally, it perfects and strengthens the bond of the recipient with the Church.

All who have been baptized but not yet confirmed should receive this sacrament. In the Latin Rite, Church law sets the age of discretion as the earliest age at which one can be confirmed. However, episcopal conferences can establish an older age for Confirmation in a particular country or region.

The ordinary minister of Confirmation in the Latin Rite is the bishop. The bishop, as minister, is a clear sign of the close bond Confirmation builds with the Church. It also visually reflects the apostolic origins of this sacrament. For serious reasons, the bishop can delegate to priests the faculty to confirm.

Again, the *Catechism of the Catholic Church* summarizes well the effects of this powerful sacrament:

> "Confirmation perfects Baptismal grace; it is the sacrament which gives the Holy Spirit in order to root us more deeply in the divine filiation, incorporate us more firmly into Christ, strengthen our bond with the Church, associate us more closely with her mission, and help us bear witness to the Christian faith in words accompanied by deeds" (No. 1316).

Eucharist

We turn our attention to the last of the sacraments of Christian initiation, the Eucharist.

In the now famous words of the Second Vatican Council, the Eucharist is "the source and the summit of the whole Christian life" (*Dogmatic Constitution on the Church*, No. 11).

> "The Eucharist is the heart and the summit of the Church's life, for in it Christ associates his Church and all her members with his sacrifice of praise and thanksgiving offered once for all on the cross to his Father; by this sacrifice he pours out the graces of salvation on his Body which is the Church" (*Catechism of the Catholic Church*, No. 1407).

The various names by which we describe this sacrament reveal different aspects of its centrality. It is Eucharist, "the" act of thanksgiving. It is the Lord's Supper, the reenactment of his last meal with his disciples. It is "the Breaking of the Bread," Christ's most intimate sharing of himself with his disciples. It is the Eucharistic Assembly of Believers. It is the Memorial of the Lord's passion, death, and resurrection. It is the Holy Sacrifice, the Sacrifice of the Mass, the Holy Liturgy. It is the Most Blessed Sacrament, Communion, Bread of Angels, Bread of Heaven. Each of these names highlight a different aspect of this sacrament.

In its essence, this sacrament is the Body and Blood of Jesus, the pledge of Jesus' love, of his presence with us, and of the certainty of his return in glory. The first disciples recognized this gift and, in accord with Jesus' command, "Do this in memory of me" (Lk 22:19), remained faithful to this "breaking of the bread." While the liturgical celebration of the Eucharist has undergone many changes over the centuries, the essential elements have remained the same, following one fundamental structure described in detail by St. Justin Martyr in the second century. Throughout its history, you can clearly distinguish the various elements: the Gathering, the Liturgy of the Word, the Preparation of the Altar, the Presentation of the Gifts, the Eucharistic Prayer, the Communion, and the Thanksgiving.

The *Catechism* explains:

"We carry out this command of the Lord by celebrating the memorial of his sacrifice. In so doing, we offer to the Father what he has himself given us: the gifts of his creation, bread and wine, which, by the power of the Holy Spirit and by the words of Christ, have become the Body and Blood of Christ. Christ is thus really and mysteriously made present" (No. 1357).

This presence of Christ is, at one and the same time, a memorial, a sacrifice, and a banquet. It is the memorial of his passion, death, and resurrection. It is a sacrifice which makes Christ's death on the cross present once again and offers the people of the present age the opportunity to associate themselves with that sacrifice. Finally, it is the banquet at which we are fed with the very Body and Blood of Christ.

How is Christ present in the Eucharist? His presence is unique. The Council of Trent explains well both the presence and the process by which Christ becomes present.

Of this presence, it says: "The body and blood, together with the soul and divinity, of our Lord Jesus Christ and, therefore, the whole Christ is truly, really, and substantially contained" (*Council of Trent*, No. 1551 [DS 1651] ND 1526).

Of the process, it declares: "Because Christ our Redeemer said that it was truly his body that he was offering under the species of bread, it has always been the conviction of the Church of God, and this holy Council now again declares that, by the consecration of the bread and wine there takes place a change of the whole substance of the bread into the substance of the Body of Christ our Lord and of the whole substance of the wine into the substance of his Blood. This change the holy Catholic Church has fittingly and properly called transubstantiation" (*Council of Trent*, No. 1551 [DS 1642] ND 1519).

In keeping with our belief regarding this presence, we strive, first of all, to show respect and reverence when in our churches, as the Eucharist is preserved there, which means Christ is present there in this unique but real way.

More, when we approach to be fed with the Eucharistic bread, we prepare ourselves in every way possible. We fast. We use special attitudes and gestures to prepare our bodies. We pray. We beg forgiveness of our sins. We forgive others. We declare ourselves to be "at peace" with our sisters and brothers, all to prepare our souls.

Catholics are encouraged to partake of the Eucharist every time that they assist at the liturgy. Complete participation in the liturgy includes being fed with the Body and Blood of Christ. While bound to assist at the liturgy every Sunday and holy day, we are by law only obliged to receive the Eucharist once a year, if possible during the Easter season.

The principal effect of receiving the Eucharist is an intimate union with Jesus. As spiritual food, this sacrament preserves, increases, and renews the life which we have through Baptism. As Jesus said clearly, "Just as the living Father sent me, and I live because of the Father, so whoever eats me will live because of me" (Jn 6:57).

The Eucharist has many other effects. It forgives venial sin. It strengthens us to avoid future sins. It motivates us to acts of charity and virtue, especially towards the poor. The Eucharist builds us more securely into the Church and unites us more closely to one another.

Because the Eucharist is a sign of unity already in existence, it is not shared with those separated from us in sacramental belief and/or ordination practice. We may, under certain circumstances, share Eucharist with Eastern churches not in full communion but preserving the sacraments of Eucharist and priesthood. However, we do not practice Eucharistic intercommunion with the Western churches derived from the Reformation or later and still separate from the Catholic Church. While lamenting our inability to signify a unity which does not yet in fact exist, we readily acknowledge that these communities do bear witness to life in communion with Christ and their expectation of his glorious return in glory when they commemorate his death and resurrection in the Lord's Supper.

These effects of the Eucharist indicate again that it is the source of our Christian life. It is also the summit. There is no clearer sign of our hope in the glorious second coming of Christ than the Eucharist. Well did St. Thomas Aquinas call it a pledge of future glory. He used the word "pledge" here in the sense of a promise of the future in which a down-payment is given at the present moment. Every time that we receive the Eucharist we strengthen our life in Christ and our confidence in reaching the summit of the Christian life which is union with him forever in heaven.

From a consideration of the sacraments of initiation, we turn to the two great sacraments of healing in the Church, Penance and the Anointing of the Sick.

Penance and Reconciliation

The sacrament of Penance, or Reconciliation, is popularly known as "confession" since an essential element of the sacrament is the admission or confession of one's sins.

This sacrament is the great healer of our sins which occur after Baptism. The frailty and weakness of our human nature, which we call "concupiscence," remains after Baptism and we do sin. Penance is the remedy for those sins.

Conversion is, in fact, part of the very life of the individual and of the Church. Christ calls us to a continual conversion of heart, starting with the first and fundamental conversion of Baptism but continuing on for a lifetime. The conversion we are called to is, first of all, an inner conversion of heart, moving us to sorrow for our sins and reconciliation with our God and others. That inner conversion is most often reflected in exterior acts of penance.

The external forms of penance in the life of the Christian can be many. The traditional forms are encompassed in the three categories of fasting, prayer and almsgiving.

Christ instituted the sacrament of Penance for all the sinful members of his Church. This institution is reflected in the words of Jesus to St. Peter,

> "I will give you the keys of the kingdom of heaven and whatever you bind on earth will be bound in heaven, and whatever you loose on earth will be loosed in heaven" (Mt 16:19).

This sacrament forgives the offense against God and restores communion of the sinner with the Church.

While the manner of administering the sacrament has varied over the ages, we can find the same fundamental structure. The acts of the penitent always include contrition, confession, and satisfaction. The action of the Church is to intervene and secure God's act of forgiveness.

Contrition can be perfect, that is, arising from the love of God above all other motives, or imperfect, that is, arising from lower motives like the fear of punishment. Confession of one's sins is an essential element. Serious sins must be confessed to a priest at least once a year according to Church law, but reception of this sacrament is encouraged on a much more frequent basis because of the multiple spiritual goods which confession brings to the individual.

Satisfaction, or penance, is an attempt to restore the disorder which sin causes in the life of the individual and of the community.

The minister of Penance is the bishop or priest. The minister acts in the name of Christ and of the Church. He is bound by the "sacramental seal" never to disclose anything he has learned in the confessional. There are no exceptions to this special bond of silence.

The spiritual effects of the sacrament of Penance are:

"reconciliation with God by which the penitent recovers grace;
reconciliation with the Church;
remission of the eternal punishment incurred by mortal sins;

remission, at least in part, of temporal punishments resulting from sin;
peace and serenity of conscience, and spiritual consolation;
an increase of spiritual strength for the Christian battle" (*Catechism of the Catholic Church*, No. 1496).

The doctrine of indulgences is closely linked to the sacrament of Penance. The merits of Jesus, which are without limit, as well as those of the Blessed Virgin Mary and the saints, are dispensed by the Church from what we call the Church's treasury. By performing meritorious acts of charity and piety, the faithful can gain indulgences for themselves and for the souls in purgatory from this spiritual treasury. These indulgences are for the remission of the temporal punishment which is due to sin and can be either partial or total.

Penance is celebrated today in the Church in one of three forms.

Individual confession to the priest and individual absolution is the most common form. The second is individual confession and absolution in the framework of a communal preparation and thanksgiving. The third, presently allowed only in cases of urgent need, is a communal celebration with a general confession and general absolution. When this third form is used, there remains the personal obligation to confess any grave sins individually when one is able.

The Anointing of the Sick

Illness and suffering have always been among the greatest burdens of human life. During his time on earth, Christ demonstrated great compassion for the sick and the ill, forgiving their sins and often physically healing them.

But Christ did not heal all of the sick. He taught us the redemptive value of suffering. By his own passion and death, he gave suffering a new value. Suffering can make us more like himself and unite us to his own redemptive suffering.

Jesus gave the power of relieving suffering and of deepening this new meaning of suffering to his disciples: "They will lay their hands on the sick and they will recover" (Mk 16:1718). The early Church carried out the exercise of this power from the very beginning. In his epistle, the apostle James says,

> "Are any among you sick? They should call for the elders of the church and have them pray over them, anointing them with oil in the name of the Lord. The prayer of faith will save the sick, and the Lord will raise them up; and anyone who has committed sins will be forgiven" (Jm 5:14-15).

Over the course of years, this sacrament began to be put off more and more until finally it was administered only during the very last moments of life when death was practically inevitable; hence, the popular name, "Extreme Unction." One of the reforms following the Second Vatican Council was the restoration of this sacrament to its rightful position. The reform *Apostolic Constitution* of November 1972 said:

> "The sacrament of the anointing of the sick is given to those who are seriously ill by anointing them on the forehead and hands with blessed olive oil or, according to circumstances, with another blessed plant oil, and saying once only these words: 'Through this holy anointing, may the Lord in his love and mercy help you with the grace of the Holy Spirit. May the Lord who frees you from sin save you and raise you up.'"

The reform document goes on to explain that the purpose of this renewal is to restore emphasis on the sacrament's being a sacrament of "the sick" and not necessarily of "the dying." Anyone who is in any danger of death because of sickness or old age can and should receive this sacrament of strengthening and comfort. A person should be anointed before a serious operation or medical treatment. This anointing can be repeated if a person recovers and falls ill again, or should a person's condition become more serious during the same illness or danger period.

The minister of the sacrament of the Anointing of the Sick is only the priest or bishop. Whenever possible, this sacrament should be celebrated in a communal setting. Ideally, it should be celebrated within the Eucharistic liturgy itself. When this is not possible, there are a variety of other settings presented in which this sacrament can take place in a communal situation. When even this is not possible, there is a much briefer form of anointing which can be used in emergencies.

The *Catechism of the Catholic Church* succinctly sets out the effects of this sacrament.

"The special grace of the sacrament of the Anointing of the Sick has as its effects:

the uniting of the sick person to the passion of Christ, for his own good and that of the whole Church;
the strengthening, peace, and courage to endure in a Christian manner the sufferings of illness or old age;
the forgiveness of sins if the sick person was not able to obtain it through the sacrament of Penance;
the restoration of health if it is conducive to the salvation of his soul;
the preparation for the passing over to eternal life" (No. 1532).

In addition to the Anointing of the Sick, the Church offers the Eucharist as viaticum (literally, supplies for a journey) to those who are about to die. The Eucharist in this setting is a special gift for the Christian on the way as he or she passes over into eternal life.

As Baptism, Confirmation, and the Eucharist constitute the sacraments of initiation into the Christian life, so Penance, the Anointing of the Sick, and the Eucharist in this special setting as viaticum complete our earthly pilgrimage and prepare us for our entrance into our heavenly home.

We now turn our attention to two sacraments which are directed toward assisting the salvation of others while contributing to personal salvation through these acts of service. These two sacraments are Orders and Marriage.

The Sacrament of Orders

Orders, through its three degrees of episcopacy, presbyterate and diaconate, continues the mission which Christ entrusted to his apostles. The name "order" comes from the Roman "ordo" which was an established civil body, especially a governing body. The act of being incorporated into any of these bodies in the Church is called "ordination." The laying on of hands accompanied by the prayer of consecration confers a gift of the Holy Spirit which permits the exercise of the sacred order.

The priesthood of the Old Testament, of Aaron, of the Levites, of the seventy elders, of Melchizedek, and countless others, was a type or prefigurement of the priesthood of the New Testament. All of these priesthoods were fulfilled in Jesus Christ. In the New Testament, all the faithful participate in the priesthood of Jesus Christ. The ministerial priesthood, while interrelated with this priesthood of the faithful, differs from it in essence and not only in degree.

Priests act in the person of Christ the head in carrying out their ministry. The Holy Spirit works in them and through them and guarantees the effectiveness of the priest in the administration of the sacraments; even the minister's sinfulness cannot impede the effect of grace. This does not mean that the minister's personal sanctity and humanity has no influence and cannot either positively or negatively affect the Church's apostolic efficacy.

The bishop represents the fullness of the priesthood. He is joined in a hierarchical communion with the other members of the episcopal college and with the head of that college, the Pope.

Priests are co-workers with the episcopal order in carrying out the mission of the Church. They are called to serve the people in one priestly college with their bishop. They form a special group, or presbyterium, around the bishop. They receive a particular office or parish to care for from his hands and thus share in his responsibility for the local Church.

Deacons are ordained to assist the bishop and priests in liturgical functions, especially the Eucharist, and in various ministries of charity. Theirs is an order of service. The Second Vatican Council restored the diaconate in the Latin Rite as a distinct and permanent rank. Married men can be ordained to this permanent diaconate.

Only validly ordained bishops can confer the three degrees of the Sacrament of Orders. In each degree, the essence of the sacrament consists in the laying on of hands by the bishop and a special consecratory prayer. The valid subject of ordination is a baptized man. In the Latin Rite, with the exception of permanent deacons, candidates for ordination normally live as celibates and pledge themselves to a lifelong observance of celibacy for the sake of the kingdom. In the Eastern Rites, while priestly celibacy is held in high regard and bishops are drawn only from the ranks of celibates, a different discipline is in effect and priests may be married.

The two proper effects of this sacrament are, first, an indelible character which is permanent and nonrepeatable and, secondly, the conferring of the grace of the Holy Spirit configuring the ordained to Christ, the priest, teacher and pastor. While for a just reason, a validly ordained man can be discharged from the obligations and rights of priesthood, or forbidden to exercise them, he remains an ordained minister of the Church forever.

The Sacrament of Marriage

Marriage in the Catholic tradition is a lifelong covenant between a man and a woman in which they pledge themselves exclusively to one another for their own mutual support and well-being and for the procreation and rearing of children.

It is significant that the Bible opens with the story of the creation of man and woman in the likeness of God and concludes with a mystical vision of the "marriage of the Lamb." In between, in both Old and New Testament, married love is lifted up as a great human blessing and as a foreshadowing of God's love for his people and his Church. God created man and woman through love and he calls them to love, and it is in and through love that they become most like himself.

It is true that this initial and ideal state of marriage suffered from sin and its effect. People experience sin within themselves, around them, and in their relationships, even in the relationship of marriage. Still, this order of creation persists and man and woman, with God's grace, are called to give themselves totally to each other in mutual help and self-giving in a lifelong covenant. From the beginning of the public life of Jesus, he and his disciples taught clearly, by word and action, the unity and indissolubility of marriage.

The parties to a sacramental marriage are a baptized man and woman, acting freely and not impeded by any natural or ecclesiastical law. The couple themselves are the ministers of marriage. By expressing their consent before the Church, they confer this sacrament on one another. It is this exchange of consent between the couple which is the indispensable element of the sacrament of Marriage. Usually, Catholics are married during the Eucharist to recall the connection of this sacrament, as well as all the other sacraments, to Christ's paschal mystery.

Even outside of the Eucharistic liturgy, the Church normally requires that the canonical form of marriage be followed. As marriage is a sacrament and a liturgical action, it is fitting that it be celebrated in the public form established by the Church. As it introduces one into an ecclesial order and creates rights and duties, as it is a public state of life, and because its public celebration protects both the sacrament and the parties entering into marriage, the celebration of marriage according to a set canonical form is most appropriate.

Because of the seriousness of the choice involved in marriage, the Church lays great stress on preparation of young people for marriage. All of a person's life, especially his or her own home life and the example of parents, makes up the remote preparation for marriage. The immediate preparation is the duty of the pastor and others entrusted with this task. This immediate preparation covers both the rights and responsibilities of marriage and is tailored to the needs of the couple. This period of preparation, both remote and proximate, is all the more important in our pluralistic society where not all hold the same view of marriage and where many marriages are entered into with a non-Catholic or even a non-Christian spouse. Differences of religious affiliation, as well as differences about the very meaning of marriage, make success in marriage that much the more of a challenge. This reality explains why special permission is needed to enter into marriage with a baptized non-Catholic Christian and a specific dispensation is required to enter into marriage with a non-baptized person.

The two chief effects of the reception of the sacrament of Marriage are a bond between the parties, which is, by its very nature, permanent and exclusive, and the bestowal of the special grace of the sacrament. The fathers of the Second Vatican Council described this special grace:

"Finally, in virtue of the sacrament of matrimony, by which they signify and share the mystery of that unity and fruitful love which exists between Christ and his Church, Christian spouses help one another to attain to holiness in their married life and in the rearing of their children. Hence, by reason of their state in life and of their position, they have their own gifts among the People of God" (*Dogmatic Constitution on the Church*, No. 11).

The fundamental task of marriage is to be at the service of life. Again, the Council fathers remind us that the institution of marriage and conjugal love are, by their very nature, directed to the begetting and upbringing of children and are crowned by it (*Pastoral Constitution on the Church in the Modern World*, No. 48).

Marriage is of utmost importance to the future of both Church and society. The basic building block of our natural society is the family. Addressing the importance of the state of marriage to the Church, the Council fathers referred to the family as a "domestic church." Within the family circle, children first hear the faith; within the family, children first practice the faith; and within the family, children first witness the faith being lived out by their parents and other members of the family. Thus, the family is truly a domestic Church, a school of Christian virtue and love.

Other Liturgical Celebrations

The new *Catechism* concludes its consideration of the celebration of the Christian mystery with a treatment of sacramentals and Christian funerals.

Sacramentals are sacred signs which bear a certain resemblance to sacraments. They are like sacraments in that they signify effects, particularly of a spiritual nature, that are obtained through the Church's prayer and intercession, and they dispose people to receive the chief effects of the sacraments. They are unlike sacraments in that they do not confer the grace of the Holy Spirit as the sacraments do. They do, however, prepare us to receive grace, and they dispose us to cooperate with it.

Sacramentals include blessings for certain ministers of the Church, for certain states of life, for certain occasions, and for certain useful objects.

Beyond the liturgy, there is another expression of the religious sense of people in the form of popular piety. This is a rich source of wisdom and insight arising from the grassroots of the Church. The Church fosters this popular piety, while at the same time remaining vigilant to clarify these popular notions in the light of faith.

As the final goal of Christian life is union with God, the Church stands by her children to the very end of the journey of life. In death, she sees the fullness of incorporation into the paschal mystery of

Christ's death and resurrection for her children. The Christian funeral does not confer any sacrament or sacramental on the deceased. He or she has moved beyond the sacramental economy. The funeral is, however, a liturgical celebration of the Church. It is an opportunity to proclaim eternal life, to proclaim the doctrine of the communion of saints, and to enable the community gathered for the funeral to share in that communion.

The order of the funeral is divided into three parts: the home or funeral parlor, the Church, and the cemetery, with the heart of the celebration being the Eucharistic liturgy in Church.

The message of the funeral celebration is that for God's faithful people, in death life is changed, not ended. As the *Catechism* concludes this second book, "For even dead, we are not at all separated from one another, because we all run the same course and we will find one another again in the same place. We shall never be separated, for we live for Christ, and now we are united with Christ as we go towards him . . . we shall all be together in Christ" (No. 1690).

(Page 83 is blank)

Book Three
Life in Christ

The third book of the *Catechism* is entitled "Life in Christ." You can see the progression. The Creed, which we considered earlier, confesses the greatness of God and his wonderful gifts to the world, especially his giving us Jesus to be our Redeemer and Sanctifier.

What that Creed confessed, the sacraments communicate. We considered the sacraments which are the means of God's giving us new life and strengthening and developing that new life.

Now, in Book Three, "Life in Christ," we are going to consider how that same faith calls us to lead a life worthy of our dignity; in other words, to live a life "in Christ." Just as Jesus always lived in the presence of the Father, and always did what was pleasing to the Father, so the Christian living in Christ is invited to strive to live always in the presence of the Father and in accord with the will of the Father.

Life in Christ: Our Human Vocation

Catechesis must be clear about both the joy and the responsibility of this life in Christ. It must be a catechesis of the Holy Spirit; of grace; of the Beatitudes; of the mystery of sin and forgiveness; of human and Christian virtues, especially the Christian virtues of faith, hope, and charity; of the two great commandments of love; of the Church. But, its alpha and its omega, its beginning and end, its centering point, must always be Jesus, who is the Way, the Truth, and the Life.

When we consider our human vocation, we begin with the foundation of our human dignity, that is, our having been created in the image and likeness of God. Christ "fully disclosed what it is to be human and manifests the nobility of our calling."

The outstanding sign of our human dignity and our having been created in the divine image is our freedom. Although wounded by original sin, each of us is obliged to follow the moral law doing what is good and avoiding what is evil. We are assisted in this struggle by the new life which we possess in the Holy Spirit because of our belief in Jesus Christ.

Jesus came to teach us the way to happiness and the true use of that gift of freedom. At the very heart of his message stands the Beatitudes:

"Blessed are the poor in spirit, for theirs is
the kingdom of heaven.
Blessed are those who mourn, for they will
be comforted.
Blessed are the meek, for they will inherit the
earth.
Blessed are those who hunger and thirst for
righteousness, for they will be filled.
Blessed are the merciful, for they will receive
mercy.
Blessed are the pure in heart, for they will
see God.
Blessed are the peacemakers, for they will be
called children of God.
Blessed are those who are persecuted for
righteousness' sake, for theirs is the kingdom
of heaven.
Blessed are you when people revile you and
persecute you and utter all kinds of evil
against you falsely on my account.
Rejoice and be glad, for your reward is great
in heaven" (Mt 5:3-10).

The Beatitudes respond to our innate desire for
happiness. They reveal to us the ultimate purpose of
our human existence. They challenge us to live with
love of God above all things as the rule of our hearts.

Sustained by the Holy Spirit, following the
commandments, the Sermon on the Mount, and the

apostles' teachings, we pursue this journey which leads to the kingdom of heaven. We live in Christ.

Freedom and the Morality of Human Acts

We said earlier that our freedom is one of the marks of our human dignity. Freedom is the power to act or not to act in accord with our own free choice. We are always free, but in accord with our own high destiny, freedom is authentic only when it serves goodness, truth, and justice.

Since it is essential to our human dignity, freedom should be protected by civil law. The society in which we live ought to strive to make it easy for us to exercise our freedom. At the same time, each individual is responsible for his or her use of this precious gift of freedom. We are responsible for our exercise of freedom.

This responsibility or imputability can be reduced or even removed by many factors, such as ignorance, fear and inadvertence, but our free, deliberately chosen acts remain our responsibility. They are our exercise of this great gift of freedom, and this exercise of freedom will either draw us closer to God (an act of virtue) or lead us away from God (an act of sin).

Thus, each of our actions has a moral value. They are either good or evil. This moral judgment of an act, that is, the judgment that it is either good or evil, depends on three factors: the object, the intention, and the circumstances.

The object chosen must be a good. When the will chooses an object, reason judges it to be good or evil. The intention, or end, must be a good. A good intention cannot make a bad act good. The end does not justify the means, but the intention, or end, in every case must be a good. Finally, the circumstances of an act, while secondary elements, do increase or diminish the moral goodness or evil of the act.

A morally good act demands that the object, the purpose, and the circumstances are all good. There are certain acts which are always morally wrong by reason of their object and can never be chosen whatever the intention and/or the circumstances.

Our choice to act or not to act is strongly influenced by our passions. Passions are affections or feelings which incline us towards what we perceive to be "the good" and away from what we perceive to be "the bad."

Chief among the passions are love and hatred, desire and fear, joy and sorrow, and anger. These passions are in themselves neither good nor evil. If guided by the reason and will, they direct us towards the good and hence they become morally good. If not controlled by the reason and the will, they direct us towards the evil and hence become morally evil. Moral goodness consists in a movement towards the good, inspired and directed by the Holy Spirit, which arises from our entire being, our reason, our will, and our passions, all working together to move us towards the good.

In the heart of each of us is a law written by God himself, a law which speaks to us in a voice we cannot silence, a voice we call "conscience." Again, our basic human dignity demands that we listen to the voice of conscience. It also requires that we try to develop this voice of conscience. We must strive to recognize the principles of morality, apply them in the concrete situations of our life, and pass judgment about the goodness or evil of actions which we have done or are contemplating doing.

Formation of conscience is no easy job. It is a lifelong task. From our earliest years, we must strive to understand and accept the principles of the moral law through our exercise of the virtue of prudence, through advice and direction which we receive from others, and through our own prayer and reflection on the Word of God. We must strive throughout life to conform our judgments to right reason and to God's wisdom.

Virtues

We are assisted in our efforts to live out our call to life in Christ by virtues, natural and theological.

A virtue is a habitual and firm disposition to do the good thing. Among the virtues, four are the hinge or "cardinal" ones as all other virtues depend on these chief virtues. These cardinal virtues are prudence, justice, fortitude, and temperance.

Prudence disposes us to choose the good in every situation and to correctly choose the steps towards the attainment of that good. Justice motivates us to render to God and to neighbor their due. Fortitude disposes us to remain constant and fixed in our pursuit of the good, even in the midst of trial and difficulty. Temperance disposes us to moderation and balance in our use of created things and in all our desires.

These are natural virtues which are intensified and purified by grace. They are based upon the three theological virtues of faith, hope, and love.

Faith is the virtue by which we believe in God because he is truth, and we believe all that he has revealed and that the Church proposes to us for belief. Hope is the virtue by which we seek the happiness of heaven and place our trust in God giving us eternal life and the means to attain it. Charity is the theological virtue by which we love

God above all things and love our neighbor as ourselves for the love of God.

Besides these dispositions to goodness, our life in Christ is assisted by the gifts of the Holy Spirit. These gifts complete and perfect the virtues. They are permanent dispositions which keep us open to the promptings of the Holy Spirit. The gifts of the Holy Spirit are: wisdom, understanding, counsel, fortitude, knowledge, piety and fear of the Lord.

It is only against this knowledge of the dignity of our call and the many aids which God gives us to walk the road of discipleship that we can understand the gravity of sin.

The Concept of Sin

Sin is any deed, word, or desire contrary to God's law. Sin is an offense against truth, reason and conscience, and a failure of love for God and neighbor.

Sins can be classified in many ways, but the most common is to divide them, in accord with their gravity, into mortal and venial sin.

Mortal sin is a serious offense against the law of God which destroys love in our hearts. Venial sin, a less serious offense, offends and wounds charity in our hearts, but does not remove it or destroy it.

For a sin to be mortal or deadly, three conditions are necessary: grave matter, full knowledge, and deliberate consent. If any of these elements is missing or diminished in any way, the sin is not mortal. If the matter is not serious, or if the knowledge is not full, or if the consent is not deliberate, the sin is venial.

Sin, especially repeated sin, dulls our conscience, weakens our judgment of good, and tends to incline us toward further sin.

A vice is the opposite of a virtue, that is, it is a habitual and firm disposition toward evil. The seven capital vices or sins according to Christian tradition are: pride, greed, envy, anger, lust, gluttony, and sloth.

Besides our own personal sins, we share in responsibility for the sins of others when we participate willingly in them; when we order, advise, or approve them; when we do not try to stop their sins when possible; or when we protect evildoers. We also share responsibility for social situations and institutions which arise contrary to God's goodness, the so-called "social sins" of our society.

The Human Person Living in Society

From a consideration of social sins, the *Catechism* turns to a consideration of the call of human society as a whole to transformation. The individual person is called to a *metanoia*, a transformation of life; so also society is called to a transformation of the human condition.

The human person is called to live in society. The union among the divine persons in the Trinity models this relationship which should exist between the individual and society. Human beings are to establish a fellowship of love and truth with one another in society. Certain societies, like the family and the state, correspond more closely with human nature's needs and are more necessary to human nature.

Society is necessary for human life. Now, some societies do present potential problems. When society threatens personal freedom and initiative, it becomes not a help to the individual human person, but a hindrance. Societies can also clash among themselves. The principle of subsidiarity demands that a higher society not usurp or restrict the internal life of a lower society. Each has its own independent sphere of activity.

All authority comes from God. Human society is invested with authority by the individuals who comprise it. Through the use of this legitimate authority, human society sets down the requirements for law and order. The exact form of government and the exact methods of selection of the leaders of a society are left to the free will of the members.

Society should seek the common good, that is,

"the sum total of social conditions enabling groups and individuals to achieve perfection more readily and completely" (*Pastoral Constitution on the Church in the Modern World*, No. 1). The common good consists of three elements: (1) respect for the person and the promotion of his or her rights, (2) the social well-being and development of the group, (3) the preservation of peace and security for all.

Individuals have the duty to assist society in this following out of the common good by both assuming personal responsibility and by participating in the public life of the society as actively as possible.

In turn, society seeks to achieve those conditions in which each person or group can obtain their due. Respect for the human person is based on the recognition of the rights which he or she possesses as a creature of God. It moves one to look on every other person as "another self" and to promote and respect the basic dignity of the "other self," especially if that other is disadvantaged or different in any way.

We must stand with, not separate from, our brothers and sisters. This principle of human solidarity is manifested in efforts to more equally distribute material goods, in striving to equalize the remuneration of labor, and, most especially, in the sharing of spiritual goods and gifts.

The Moral Law and Grace

In our quest for happiness, God assists us by his gifts of law and grace.

Law is a rule of conduct set down by the competent authority for the sake of the common good. There are several different expressions of law.

The moral law is God's wisdom at work within us and within all creation. The expressions of this moral law are many, but they all coalesce into the one law of God.

We speak of the eternal law which is the source of all in God himself. We also speak of the natural law which is found within creation. It is a sharing in the wisdom and the goodness of God bestowed on human creation. Natural law is a special gift of God through which we know the good we ought to do and the evil we ought to avoid. This natural law is based on the fundamental dignity of the human person. It is the basis of human rights and duties. While its expression may vary throughout history, the natural law is unchangeable and permanent. While not perceived immediately and clearly by all, it remains the basis of all law.

We speak of the "Old Law" which was God's revelation of himself to his people chronicled in the Old Testament. This law, the first stage of revelation and a preparation for the Gospel, was imperfect. It was not complete in itself but was a preparation for the fullness of revelation which was to come in and through Jesus.

The "New Law," revealed through the Gospels, is the perfection here on earth of the divine law, both natural and revealed. It is the fulfillment and completion of the Old Law. This New Law is a law of love, of grace, and of freedom. We find this New Law summed up in the Sermon on the Mount. This New Law aims at the reformation of all our acts at their very roots, that is, in the midst of the human heart. It is a law of love — love of God with all our powers and love of our neighbor as we love ourselves.

The New Law also introduces the evangelical counsels. These evangelical counsels reach beyond the law and motivate us toward the rejection not only of those things which are contrary to Christian love, but even of those objects which in any way impede the perfect growth and development of Christian love within our souls.

We are justified not through our observance of the law but by the grace of the Holy Spirit given to us in Baptism. This justification has been merited for each of us by the suffering and death of Christ.

Grace is the name we give to this free and undeserved help which God gives us, empowering us to respond to his call and to become his adopted sons and daughters, sharing in his own divine nature.

We distinguish different types of grace. We speak of sanctifying grace which is a habitual gift, a stable and supernatural disposition which renders the soul capable of living with God and of acting in accord with his love. We also speak of habitual grace which is a permanent disposition to live and act in accordance with God's law. We distinguish habitual grace from actual grace, which is divine intervention which comes at various times in the course of one's life, a "grace of the moment."

All of these graces are God's free gifts. We cannot earn them in any way. We are unable without his help to merit initial grace. The love of Christ is the source of all our merits before God.

This spiritual progress reaches its perfection in a mystical union with Christ. This intimate union is called mystical because it shares in the mystery of Christ and in the mystery of the Trinity itself.

At whatever stage of the spiritual journey we find ourselves, we realize that the way of perfection is the way of the cross. Like Jesus himself we must expect self-denial and sacrifice to be the stepping stones to sanctity and perfection for ourselves.

The Church, Mother and Teacher

The Church is the mother and teacher, the model and the guide, of the effort of the individual member to live out God's law of love. The Church lives out the command she received from the apostles to be the "pillar and bulwark" of truth (1 Tm 3:15). She presents, applies, and interprets the original deposit of faith to succeeding generations.

We call this teaching voice of the Church her "Magisterium." Although one voice, we distinguish two expressions of the teaching voice of the Church. We distinguish the extraordinary from the ordinary teaching voice of the Church.

The extraordinary teaching voice of the Church, which concerns the explanation of the deposit of faith and those elements of doctrine essential to the safeguarding of the faith, participates so closely in the authority of Christ that it is protected from error by the special gift of infallibility. This exercise of Magisterium demands acceptance by all members of the Church.

The ordinary teaching voice of the Church, extending beyond the original deposit of faith and the essential elements of the faith, also calls for loving acceptance by the membership of the Church. Since it is the Church which through Baptism has given us new life in Christ and made us members of his Body, Christians should have a true filial love for the Church.

In fulfilling her teaching office, the Church has set down in her precepts the minimum requirements for membership and for growth in God's love. These six precepts as presented in the new *Catechism* are: (1) to attend Mass on Sunday and feast days, (2) to receive the Sacrament of Reconciliation at least once a year, (3) to receive Holy Communion during the Easter time, (4) to keep holy the feast days of obligation, (5) to fast and abstain on the appointed days, (6) to contribute to the support of the Church.

You will note that this official listing is slightly different than the listing that most of us learned when we studied the *Baltimore Catechism*. That is because the list in the *Baltimore Catechism* was a list adopted by the Third Council of Baltimore but not an officially promulgated version of the precepts of the Church for the faithful everywhere.

These precepts are further specifications of the great commandment of love of God and neighbor. They complement and complete the Decalogue (ten words) or Ten Commandments given by God to Moses. The Church considers these ten rules or laws to be of fundamental importance to the Christian life. The numbering of the Ten Commandments has varied in the course of history, but the content remains the same.

Traditionally, we speak of a division of the Ten Commandments into two tablets or sections. The first three commandments deal with our obligation of love of God; the last seven concern our obligation of love toward our neighbor.

We will consider each of these commandments

individually. Here, let us set them forth briefly. Certainly these are ten rules of life which each of us ought to know by rote — and live out instinctively in our daily life.

THE TEN COMMANDMENTS

1. I am the Lord your God; you shall not have strange gods before me.
2. You shall not take the name of the Lord your God in vain.
3. Remember to keep holy the Lord's day.
4. Honor your father and your mother.
5. You shall not kill.
6. You shall not commit adultery.
7. You shall not steal.
8. You shall not bear false witness against your neighbor.
9. You shall not covet your neighbor's wife.
10. You shall not covet your neighbor's goods.

Knowing these commandments well is the essential first step to living them well!

I am the Lord your God;
you shall not have strange gods before me.

The first commandment is an echo of the well-known "Shema Israel" prayer of Deuteronomy, "Hear, O Israel: the Lord is our God, the Lord alone" (Dt 6:4). This first commandment calls upon us to place our faith, trust, and hope in God alone, whom we love above all things. The practice of these three theological virtues of faith, hope and charity, leads us to the act of worship of God, the first act of the virtue of religion.

The virtue of religion moves us to recognize God's position in our life, to offer prayer and sacrifice to him, and to fulfill the promises and vows which we make to him. All people have a natural right flowing from the essential dignity of the human person to express their religious beliefs in public and in private. This religious liberty is not indifference or recognition of error but rather recognition of the natural dignity of the human person.

Turning to the negative side of this first commandment, we can see that those actions which give the honor and worship due to God to other persons or objects (idolatry) are forbidden. Polytheism, the recognition of many gods, is also forbidden by this commandment. Likewise, all forms of divination, which falsely claim to reveal the future, and the practice of magic and/or sorcery, which claim to tame occult powers and put them at the disposition of humans, are likewise contrary to the first commandment.

Also forbidden by this first commandment are those sins which would violate the virtue of religion. Examples of these would be putting God to the test, sacrilege, which is the profanation of religious actions, things, or persons, and simony, which is the buying and selling of spiritual goods.

Finally, the first commandment condemns those who claim that God does not exist (atheism) or that an intimate and personal relationship with God is not possible for a human being. A step removed from atheism but also to be rejected is agnosticism which declares that the existence of God is incapable of being affirmed or denied. The position of the agnostic is that nothing can be said about God.

While we cannot represent God in any form known to humans, God does allow the use of figures and images which symbolically represent the salvation offered through his divine Son. In the Old Testament, we find God approving of the use of images to convey this representation, such as the bronze serpent and the ark of the covenant.

With the New Testament and the assumption of a human nature by the Son, a new economy of images of God was introduced, so the veneration of images of Christ, the Blessed Virgin Mary, the saints, and angels has become part of our religious expression. These images are not venerated in themselves but rather they direct us toward the reality which the image presents.

*You shall not take the name
of the Lord your God in vain.*

The second commandment is another expression of the virtue of religion. This commandment demands respect for the use of the Lord's name. We must respect God's name, use it only in a proper and suitable manner, and be ready to publicly profess our fidelity to that name. This respect, proper use, and confession extends to Jesus, to the Blessed Virgin Mary, and to the saints of the Church.

If we use God's name to bolster a promise or as a pledge of the truth, we should be careful to respect the promise we made or to state the truth in all clarity.

On the negative side, the second commandment forbids blasphemy, which is speaking evil or hatefully about God or using his name in a manner or context which reflects a lack of respect. Likewise, it would be blasphemous to use God's name to attempt to justify a criminal activity.

More than deliberate blasphemy, the ordinary Christian needs to struggle against the careless and casual use of God's name. Our culture makes this misuse of God's name acceptable and all too ordinary.

The second commandment also enjoins us to be most careful in the taking of oaths. An oath is the calling upon the truthfulness of God himself as witness to the truth contained in our own statements. Oaths are not to be used casually or in a trivial manner. For serious and just reasons, an oath may be used. Examples of such justified situations would be the oath taken as a witness in court or in the assumption of a significant office of public trust. Perjury, the utterance of a falsehood under oath, is a serious lack of respect for God's name.

As God's name demands appropriate respect, so does the name of each person. A name is a very precious gift. God has called each of us by name. That name represents the dignity of the person as well as the intimate relationship of love which exists between God the Father and his son or daughter. Our Christian name received in Baptism is to remain with us for all eternity.

It is Christian practice to bestow on a newborn the name of a saint, thus presenting the individual with a model of life and assuring the patronage of that saint towards the newborn. This baptismal name could also express a Christian virtue or mystery. Above all else, it should be a Christian name. In the naming of a baptismal candidate, care should be taken to bestow a name which reflects our Christian teaching and tradition.

Remember to keep holy the Lord's day.

The third commandment marks one day of each week as special in the relationship which exists between God and his people.

In the Old Testament, the Sabbath day recalled creation, served as a memorial of the deliverance of the Lord's people from slavery in Egypt, and stood as a sign of the covenant which existed between God and his people.

In the New Covenant, Sunday replaced the Sabbath. Jesus rose from the dead on Sunday, making this day now special in that relationship between God and his people. The observance of Sunday as the Lord's day marked the new creation and the new covenant established through Jesus' life, passion, death, and resurrection.

The Sunday Eucharist is the very heart of the life of the Church. The Second Vatican Council describes the Eucharist as the source and the summit of the whole work of preaching the Gospel and the very heartbeat of the congregation of the faithful (*Decree on the Ministry and Life of Priests*, No. 5).

For this reason, unless we have a serious excuse, all Catholics are obliged to take part in the

Eucharistic celebration on Sunday and the other holy days of the Church. This obligation can be satisfied by assisting at a liturgy celebrated anywhere in any Catholic rite, either on the day itself or on the evening of the previous day at a special vigil Mass. Ideally, however, this participation should take place in one's own parish with the community of the faithful of which one is a regular member. "A parish is a definite community of the Christian faithful established on a stable basis within a particular church; the pastoral care of the parish is entrusted to a pastor as its own shepherd under the authority of the diocesan bishop" (*Catechism of the Catholic Church*, No. 2179).

The holy days of the universal Church are ten in number: Christmas, Epiphany, Ascension, Corpus Christi, New Year's Day (Mary, Mother of God), Immaculate Conception, Assumption, St. Joseph, Sts. Peter and Paul, and All Saints. Episcopal conferences can suppress holidays or transfer them to a Sunday. In the United States, we have done so with the Epiphany, Corpus Christi, St. Joseph, and Sts. Peter and Paul. Also, when holy days fall on a Saturday or a Monday, the obligation to attend Mass can and often is dispensed.

Besides attendance at the liturgy, Sundays and holy days should be observed, as far as possible, as days of rest. These are days on which we should concentrate on worship, on works of charity and mercy toward our neighbor, on family life, and on relaxation of mind and body.

The *Catechism* sums up the Catholic's attitude toward the Sunday rest in two brief paragraphs:

> "On Sundays and other holy days of obligation, the faithful are bound . . . to abstain from those labors and business concerns which impede the worship to be rendered to God, the joy which is proper to the Lord's Day, or the proper relaxation of mind and body" (No. 2193).
> "Every Christian should avoid making unnecessary demands on others that would hinder them from observing the Lord's Day" (No. 2195).

Honor your father and your mother.

The first three commandments dealt with our obligation to love God. The next seven specify our obligation to love our neighbor.

The first of these designations deals with our parents. We are commanded to honor those who gave us the precious gift of life. The respect and obligation called for by this commandment extends to all family relationships, to all activities in which we are subject to legitimate authority.

A mother and father, together with their children, united in marriage form the family, the basic building block of both Church and civil society.

For the Church, the family, as a communion of

persons, is an image and reflection of the communion that exists among the three persons of the Blessed Trinity. As a community of faith, hope, and love, the family has special importance in the transmission and the living out of the faith. Rightly is it recognized as "the domestic Church."

For society, the family is the original cell. It supplies the members of society. It forms those members in the basic moral values necessary for society to even exist. Society's role is to support and strengthen the family and to offer assistance to families when they encounter obstacles or problems whose solutions reach beyond their singular resources.

The fourth commandment supplies us with insight into the duties of children, parents, civil authorities, citizens. In a word, it extends to all the relationships of our lives.

Children owe a special respect (filial piety) to their parents for the gift of life, for loving and nurturing them in their early years, for enabling them to grow, learn, and develop. As long as the child lives at home, he or she should obey the parents. This duty of obedience ceases when the child reaches independence and maturity, but the duty to love and respect remains. Especially should children be ready to offer their parents moral and material assistance as the parents age.

Parents, in turn, owe a special duty to their

children. They have the primary responsibility for the education of their children. They begin this education in the home, teaching and modeling all the virtues. They guide this education as it moves forward. Parents are the first heralds of faith for their children and should instruct them, again, by word and example in the life of the Church. They should respect and encourage their children's choice of a vocation in life, recalling that the first vocation of every Christian is to follow Jesus.

Our relationships in society are also part of the scope of the fourth commandment.

Those who exercise civil authority ought to see it always as a service which they render to others, respecting the fundamental rights of the persons whom they serve, especially those who are the least able to care for themselves or protect their own human dignity.

Those subject to authority should recognize their superiors as God's representatives, people who share in the authority of God himself. They should seek to contribute in accord with their individual gifts and position in life to the common good of society. This contribution is reflected in such activities as voting, paying taxes, and sharing in the defense of their society.

Unjust and oppressive political power can be opposed, even overthrown, but resort to force is justified only when strict conditions are met. These are:

1. The violation of fundamental human rights must be certain, serious, and prolonged.
2. All other means of redress must have been exhausted.
3. Resort to force should not provoke worse disorders.
4. There should be a well-founded hope of success.
5. There is no other reasonable solution at hand.

The Church is not identified in any way with political society. She stands independent. But as the *Pastoral Constitution on the Church in the Modern World* reminds us, ". . . it is always and everywhere legitimate for her (the Church) to preach the faith with true freedom, to teach her social doctrine, and to discharge her duty among men without hindrance. She also has the right to pass moral judgments, even on matters touching the political order whenever basic personal rights for the salvation of souls make such judgments necessary. In so doing, she may use only those helps which accord with the Gospel and with the general welfare as it changes according to time and circumstances" (No. 76).

You shall not kill.

God himself is the author, the sustainer, and the goal of every human life. For this reason, every human life is sacred. Each person lives in a special relationship to God.

The intentional killing of an innocent person is forbidden. Both the Old and the New Testament are filled with references to the dignity of the human person and the inviolability of human life.

Legitimate defense of society and of one's own life allows one to take the life of another when necessary. This legitimate defense can even become a duty for those charged with responsibility for the lives of others or with protecting the common good.

Society has the right to protect itself from unjust aggressors. The Church acknowledges the right and duty of the State to punish wrongdoers, even to put them to death in cases of most serious offenses. The death penalty is, however, a last resort to be used only when human life can be protected and public peace promoted adequately by no lesser penalty.

The fifth commandment forbids willful murder and forbids placing any action which intends indirectly the death of another person. It also forbids risking one's own life without serious, justifying reason.

In our society, abortion is one of the frequent

crimes against the fifth commandment. The Church teaches that human life must be protected from the moment of conception. Those who procure abortion or formally cooperate in abortion are punished with the canonical penalty of excommunication. This penalty aims at making clear the serious and irreparable damage caused by this action.

Prenatal diagnostic techniques must respect the life of the embryo or fetus and be directed to healing or protecting them. Any medical intervention must have the same goal and must not entail disproportionate risks.

Throughout the life spectrum, those who are sick or handicapped deserve special help and acceptance from their sisters and brothers so that they might lead as normal a life as possible. And when the end of life approaches, direct euthanasia is morally unacceptable.

No one is obliged to continue medical treatments which are unnecessarily burdensome, dangerous, extraordinary, or disproportionate to the hoped for outcome. In our high-tech society, durable power of attorney and living wills can adequately provide for these situations and are highly recommended.

As we are stewards even of our own gift of life, we are obliged to take reasonable care of our physical and mental health. Temperance moves us to avoid all excesses in food, alcohol, tobacco, and medicines. It likewise motivates us not to endanger our life unnecessarily by any activity. Participation in scientific, medical, or psychological experimentation is legitimate only if the risks are not disproportionate and if the consent of the subject is voluntary and fully informed. Organ transplants are moral and meritorious if the risks to the donor are proportionate to the good sought for the recipient.

As we are only stewards of the gift of life, we cannot directly and deliberately end our life through suicide. This action violates the commandment of love of self, love of neighbor, and love of God. While objectively a grave moral wrong, the responsibility of the person who has committed suicide is quite often diminished or removed by psychiatric, psychological, or other causes.

Even after death, the body must be treated with respect. The burial of the dead in the hope of the resurrection is a corporal work of mercy. Cremation is allowed provided it is reverent and does not express a denial of faith in the resurrection of the dead.

Anger and hatred destroy peace among individuals and nations and often are the precursors of the unjust taking of life. Peace is not merely the absence of war. It consists in recognizing the dignity of the person, the safeguarding of their goods, their free communication, and the constant practice of solidarity.

While forbidding the willful destruction of human life, the Church recognizes the rights of governments to legitimate self-defense. The traditional elements in the Church's just war theory are: (1) the damage inflicted by the aggressor would be serious, lasting, and certain; (2) all other means of putting an end to the war have been shown to be ineffective or impractical; (3) there must be a reasonable hope of success; (4) the use of arms must not involve more serious evils than those which are hoped to be eliminated through the waging of the war.

This whole theory of just war is being discussed in the Church, especially in the light of the tremendous changes in waging of war that have been brought about by modern technology.

Even if a just defensive war is undertaken, provision must be made for those who, as conscientious objectors, refuse to bear arms, and in the conduct of such a war, noncombatants, wounded, and prisoners are to be treated humanely.

You shall not commit adultery.

In creating man and woman, God gave them the vocation to love and to communion. God created them, male and female. Each of us is called to integrate our sexuality into our entire life, acting in freedom and with conscious choice. Each of us is called to live a life of chastity in accord with our own vocation and situation in life.

The virtue of chastity is related to the cardinal virtue of temperance. Living a chaste life is both a moral virtue and a gift from God.

Offenses against chastity include the following: lust, the disordered desire or unbridled abandonment to sexual pleasure; masturbation, the deliberate stimulation of the genital organs in order to derive sexual pleasure; fornication, sexual intercourse between an unmarried man and woman; pornography, the display of erotic or sexual acts intended to excite prurient feelings; prostitution, the paying for sexual activity with others; rape, the forceful violation of the sexual intimacy with another.

Homosexuality refers to a person's sexual orientation. Homosexuals are those who have an exclusive or predominant attraction to persons of the same sex. The Church teaches that such sexual orientation is not sinful. Individuals with this sexual orientation are to be accepted. Every mark of discrimination against them is to be avoided, but homosexual acts are "intrinsically disordered" (*Persona Humana*, No. 8). Homosexual persons are called to live a life of chastity in accord with their position and state in life as are all their sisters and brothers.

Human sexuality is expressed fully and completely in the love of a man and woman in marriage. These acts are a source of joy and goodness.

"The acts within marriage by which the intimate and chaste union of the spouses takes place are noble and honorable; the truly human performance of these acts fosters the mutual self-giving they signify and enriches the spouses in joy and gratitude" (*Pastoral Constitution on the Church in the Modern World*, No. 49).

The marriage covenant calls both spouses to a lifelong, exclusive and indissoluble union. This union achieves the twofold end of marriage which is the procreation of children and the mutual good of the spouses. From this covenant flows the duty of the spouses to be faithful to one another for life and to be open to the generation of new life through their sexual union.

The regulation of human birth by the couple for just reasons is not forbidden provided such regulation is achieved by natural means, such as the various forms of periodic continence based on the use of infertile periods for sexual union.

In a succinct paragraph, the new *Catechism* sums up the intrinsic evil of artificial birth control:

> "Thus the innate language that expresses the total reciprocal self-giving of husband and wife is overlaid, through contraception, by an objectively contradictory language, namely, that of not giving oneself totally to the other. This

leads not only to a positive refusal to be open to life but also to a falsification of the inner truth of conjugal love, which is called upon to give itself in personal totality. . . . The difference, both anthropological and moral, between contraception and recourse to the rhythm of the cycle . . . involves in the final analysis two irreconcilable concepts of the human person and of human sexuality" (No. 2370).

Research aimed at overcoming human infertility is acceptable provided it serves the human person and respects the rights of the human person, and is in accord with the plan of God. With the rapid strides of research, this field introduces complex moral dilemmas to be solved by consulting approved moral theologians.

Adultery, divorce, polygamy, and incest are serious offenses against the dignity of marriage.

You shall not steal.

The seventh commandment forbids the unjust taking or damaging of the goods or property of another.

We are all merely stewards of the goods of creation. The ownership of goods is a legitimate goal. It helps one meet basic needs, ensures the freedom and dignity of the individual, and helps meet the responsibilities which one has for the care of others. This ownership in society is subject to the regulation of the rights of ownership established by legitimate authority.

The seventh commandment forbids all taking of the property of others against their reasonable will. The respect of the property of others is part of the virtue of justice. We speak about commutative justice which regulates exchanges between persons, legal justice which regulates the obligations of an individual toward the community, and distributive justice which deals with the obligations of the community to its citizens.

Part of the restoration of justice violated by a sin against the seventh commandment demands that stolen goods be returned to their rightful owner.

As part of her mission, the Church is called upon to make moral judgments about economic and social matters when these issues affect the fundamental rights of people or the salvation of souls. We refer to these judgments as "the social teaching of the Church."

In her social teaching, the Church proposes principles for reflection, criteria for judgment, and guidelines for actions. Any economic system must be in accord with the moral order and social justice. Work is the right of every person. Through work, a person develops his or her own gifts, provides for his or her needs and those of the family, and contributes to the good of society. By work, a person shares in the action of creation itself. United to Christ, work can be truly redemptive. A special burden of concern for the functioning and the effect of the economic system falls on the government and on business leaders. And on the international level, rich nations bear a special moral responsibility toward the poorer and undeveloped nations.

The Church's moral teaching sets forth the principles, criteria, and guidelines, but the prime movers in political and social life are to be the laity. They are to strive to introduce Christian values into political and social life.

Part of the constant tradition of the Church's social teaching is a special love for the poor, a "preferential option" for them. Almsgiving to the poor is both an exercise of justice and a witness to society. The Church lists seven spiritual works of mercy and seven corporal works of mercy. These are charitable actions through which we come to the need of our neighbor and supply his or her wants, physical and spiritual.

The spiritual works of mercy are: (1) to admonish the sinner, (2) to instruct the ignorant, (3) to counsel the doubtful, (4) to comfort the sorrowful, (5) to bear wrongs patiently, (6) to forgive all injuries, (7) to pray for the living and the dead.

The corporal works of mercy are: (1) to feed the hungry, (2) to give drink to the thirsty, (3) to clothe the naked, (4) to visit the imprisoned, (5) to shelter the homeless, (6) to visit the sick, (7) to bury the dead.

> *You shall not bear false witness*
> *against your neighbor.*

The eighth commandment forbids all misrepresentation of the truth. God himself is Truth, therefore, his people are called to live in the truth. Jesus promised to send his disciples the Spirit of Truth to be with them always.

Human beings tend naturally toward truth. It would be impossible for society to function if the majority of its members were not truthful and trustworthy. This virtue of truth maintains a just balance, however, between what ought to be expressed and what ought to be kept secret. It strives to give every person his or her due.

Christians are called to give witness to the truth. By the way they speak and live, followers of Christ are called upon to witness to the Gospel and to its truth. While this witness is part of ordinary life, the supreme witness to the truth of the faith is found in the act of martyrdom, that is, in giving up one's life for the faith.

The eighth commandment forbids false witness, that is, a statement contrary to the truth before a court, as well as perjury, which is a false witness made under oath. It likewise forbids rash judgment as well as detraction, which is the disclosure of the failures of others without sufficient reason, and calumny, which is damaging the reputation of another by making untruthful statements.

The most direct offense against the truth is lying. A lie is speaking a falsehood with the intention of deceiving someone who has the right to the truth. The seriousness of each lie is determined by the nature of the truth which it distorts, the circumstances, the intention of the person who tells it, and the injury which the lie causes to the victim and others. Again, the very nature of this offense demands that restitution be made.

Love of truth and concern for the truth should inform every response we make to requests for information or communication, but not everyone has an unconditional right to the truth.

The sacramental seal of the sacrament of Reconciliation is inviolable despite the circumstances or the consequences. There is no exception.

Professional confidences, such as those shared with lawyers, doctors, psychologists, etc., must be kept except in the most serious situations when a serious and proportionate reason exists for the disclosure of the truth.

In our modern society, the means of communications play a major role in presenting truth. Along with the right to disseminate truth goes a complementary obligation that the truth conveyed be objective and that the demands of justice and charity be respected. This places a heavy responsibility on our means of social communication.

Truth is beautiful in and of itself. The fine arts, and especially sacred art, should highlight and develop that transcendental goodness of truth, giving praise, honor, and glory to God who is the source of all truth.

You shall not covet your neighbor's wife.

The ninth commandment and the tenth commandment form a unit. They both speak of concupiscence, that is, the activity of the sensory appetites against human reason. This movement is a consequence of original sin and while not sinful in itself, inclines us to sin. The ninth commandment forbids giving in to carnal concupiscence while the tenth forbids coveting the goods of others.

We commonly locate the seat of our emotions and moral actions in the heart. Thus, we speak of those who are completely in tune with God as being "pure of heart." The pure of heart are those who accord their lives with God's plan in three areas: love or charity, chastity or sexual integrity, and truth or orthodoxy of faith.

When we were baptized, we were purified from all sin, but because of the effects of

123

concupiscence, we must struggle throughout life against sin. In this struggle, our chief weapons are the virtue of chastity, purity of intention and regard, and prayer.

Maintaining purity of heart demands modesty. Modesty, which is part of the virtue of temperance, guards a person's privacy. While modesty expresses itself differently in different cultures, it is essential to this purity of heart which every Christian must seek. In our culture, modesty is a virtue little respected. In fact, our culture belittles the worth of this important virtue.

For our own sake and for the sake of the community, we are called to work for the restoration of this virtue of modesty in our social climate and in our communications media.

You shall not covet your neighbor's goods.

The tenth commandment flows from the ninth and completes it. It forbids coveting the goods of others. It speaks to the intentions of our heart which are the forerunners of our actions.

The tenth commandment calls on us to keep our sensory appetites under the control of our intellect and will. It motivates us to resist the desire for unlimited possessions, for power, and for the goods which belong to others.

The expression of a violation against this commandment often takes the form of envy. Envy is sorrow or sadness caused by seeing the possessions of others, linked with an unjust desire to appropriate these possessions for ourselves. The Christian antidote for envy is the exercise of the virtue of kindness.

The conclusion of the Vatican Council's *Dogmatic Constitution on the Church* in its treatment of the call of the whole Church to holiness serves as an apt summary of these two commandments:

> "Therefore, all the faithful are invited and bound to pursue holiness and the perfection of their own state in life. Accordingly, let all of them see that they direct their affections rightly, lest they be hindered in their pursuit of perfect love by the way they use worldly things and by an adherence to riches which is contrary to the spirit of evangelical poverty, following the Apostle's advice: let those who make use of this world not fix their abode in it, for the form of this world is passing away" (No. 42).

Book Four
Christian Prayer

We now turn our attention to Book Four of
the *Catechism of the Catholic Church*,
"Christian Prayer."

The individual Catholic professes, celebrates,
and lives his or her life of faith. That was the
message of the first three books of the *Catechism*.
In this fourth book, we turn our attention
to the close, personal, intimate relationship with
God which results from that profession,
celebration, and life of faith. We name
this special relationship "prayer."

Prayer

Prayer is the lifting up of our hearts and minds to God. It is the response of the whole person — soul, spirit, heart and body — to this personal friendship with God.

God opens this dialogue. God first calls each of us to this special relationship of prayer. It is always his free gift. Each of us, in response to God's call, is involved in the continuing search for intimacy with him.

The history of prayer is bound up with human history. Human history is the story of the relationship between God and his people.

From the Genesis story, which presented the close friendship of God and his creatures before the fall, the story of history is the story of prayer.

Events of the Old Testament reveal this history of prayer, especially in the lives of the great leaders of God's people. Prayer was paramount in the lives of Abraham, our father in faith; Jacob, the father of the twelve tribes of Israel; Moses, who led God's people to the chosen land; and in the lives of Elijah and the prophets. The importance of prayer is clearest in the life of David, the great king and author of many of the psalm prayers. Prayer in the Old Testament reaches its high point in the psalms. The psalms reveal the call of God and his people's response as individuals and as a community. They also demonstrate God's faithfulness to his promises of the past and look forward eagerly to the coming of the promised Messiah.

The great story of prayer reaches its perfection in Jesus. Jesus prayed always. He prayed in public and in private. He prayed before the decisive moments of his life. He prayed in moments of joy and in sorrow. He shared his prayer with others, especially his own disciples. He even taught others how to pray.

This story of prayer was fulfilled and brought to completion in the crucifixion, death, and resurrection of Jesus. In these events, the Father accepted the prayers of Jesus and responded to them by raising his Son from the dead.

St. Augustine beautifully summarizes Jesus' life of prayer:

> "He prays for us as our priest, prays in us as our head, and is prayed to by us as our God. Therefore let us acknowledge our voice in him and his in us" (*En. in Ps.* 85, 1).

The prayer of the Blessed Virgin Mary, especially as revealed in the Annunciation and her great prayer of praise of God uttered in that encounter, the "Magnificat," exemplifies for us the generous offering of total self to God in faith which should characterize our prayer life and our every prayer.

When the Holy Spirit descended upon the

apostles at Pentecost, a new chapter in the story of prayer opened. The Holy Spirit, promised by Jesus to teach everything and recall all that he had said, instructs and motivates the Church in her life of prayer.

Forms of Prayer and the Tradition of Prayer

The forms of prayer developed in the early Church from Old and New Testament sources remain normative for Christian prayer today.

We pray in blessing and adoration of God. We pray in petition, especially for the forgiveness of our sins. We pray in intercession, asking gifts and graces for others. We pray in thanksgiving, in the face of every event and need of life, and we pray in praise, recognizing most immediately that God is God, to be acknowledged in an unselfish manner.

All forms of prayer are contained and expressed in the Eucharist which is "the" sacrifice of praise.

To pray well, one must combine the desire to pray with learning how to pray. For the Christian, the Holy Spirit teaches these lessons of prayer through the living tradition of the Church.

The sources for our prayer life are many. Chief among these sources are the following. We have the Word of God in which we come to a knowledge of Jesus Christ and grow in friendship and personal conversation with him. We have the liturgy of the Church which both makes present and communicates the mystery of salvation. We possess the theological virtues which help to begin, sustain, and make our prayer fruitful. Faith is a doorway through which we enter into prayer. Hope sustains and nourishes our prayer in every circumstance of life. Charity draws everything into the love of God and enables us to love others as God loves us.

The language of prayer changes with each historic, social, and cultural context in which the Church finds herself, but there is essentially no other way of prayer than Christ.

We pray to the Father, but we pray to the Father through Jesus who is our access to the Father.

We pray to Jesus. That name which he received at the Incarnation contains all that the Son of God is. The simplest formulation of prayer of faith in Jesus, handed down from tradition, is this: "Lord Jesus Christ, Son of God, have mercy on us sinners." This prayer opens our heart to the grace of God's Son.

We pray to the Holy Spirit. It is the Holy Spirit's initial grace which enables us to pray at all, and it is the Spirit who leads us along the path of prayer.

Because of Mary's unique cooperation with the grace of the Holy Spirit, we pray to her as a model of prayer and as the Mother of God. As Mother of the Church, we look to Mary as the perfect "pray-er." In

our prayer to her, we praise the Lord for his goodness and entrust our prayer to the Mother of Jesus,
confident that she will intercede on our behalf.

The lives of those who have preceded us into
the kingdom, especially those recognized by the
Church as saints, offer us guidance and example for
our own life of prayer. In this living Tradition of the
Church, many different spiritualities have been developed. In their rich diversity, they show forth the
one guiding light of the Holy Spirit.

The primary place for education in prayer is
the Christian family. The family is the "domestic
Church" where children are initiated into the life of
prayer and schooled in perseverance in prayer.

Other educators in prayer are ordained ministers of the Church, men and women who have
entered consecrated life in the Church, catechists,
members of prayer groups, and spiritual directors.
All of these, provided that they draw from the
authentic wellsprings of Christian prayer, offer
guidance and assistance within the Church to those
who wish to learn and advance in the practice of
prayer.

As to the place of prayer, we can pray anywhere. Some locations are more suitable. Among
these, the preeminent place is the church. Other
suitable locations would include a monastery, a
shrine, or place of a pilgrimage. For personal private
prayer at home, a "prayer corner" with a Bible

and/or suitable religious symbols can be an aid and an impetus to prayer.

The Life of Prayer

The life of prayer has to be regular for each of us. To assist us in this life of prayer, the Church presents certain rhythms for our life: daily prayers, consisting of morning and evening prayer, grace before and after meals, and the liturgy of the hours; weekly prayers, participation in the Eucharist; yearly cycles of prayer, participation in the liturgical and sanctoral cycle of feasts.

Our personal prayer is expressed in three major forms, although each of these forms may be many and varied in their methods.

There is vocal prayer which unites our soul and our body as we express our prayer in words, mental or vocal, and pray with our whole being.

There is meditation in which the mind seeks to understand the essence of the Christian life using thought, imagination, and emotions. Aided by Christian books, above all the Scriptures, we seek to open our own "book of life" to apply the great truths of our faith to our daily living experience.

There is mental prayer which St. Teresa describes as "simply a friendly exchange and a frequent solitary conversation with him who, as we know, loves us" (*The Life of Saint Teresa of Avila*). Mental prayer seeks to transcend these other forms of prayer and to reach an intimate union with the prayer of Christ himself through contemplation.

Prayer is a gift from God, but it also demands a determined response on our part.

In our struggle to pray, we must avoid erroneous notions of just what prayer is, notions that dilute the true meaning of prayer. We have to try to avoid being affected by the attitudes of the secular world in which we live. We have to accept and struggle through our failures in prayer.

We also have to work our way through recurring difficulties in prayer, chief of which are distractions while at prayer and dryness or lack of feeling for the art of prayer.

We wrestle simultaneously with temptations which confront us in prayer, chief of which are a lack of faith or an apathy or depression at prayer.

In our prayer we strive for a childlike trust that our prayers will be heard and that these prayers will be efficacious. We strive to persevere in prayer. We let our prayer life be guided by three enlightening and lifegiving truths about prayer.

1. It is always possible to pray everywhere and in any situation.
2. Prayer is a vital and absolute necessity in our lives.
3. Prayer and the Christian life center

around the same love of God and are inseparable in our life.

The "Our Father," Part I

As a conclusion to our consideration of Christian prayer, we look closely at the "Our Father," the prayer which Jesus himself taught us.

The Lord's Prayer has been described by Christian tradition as "the summary of the whole Gospel" (Tertullian), the "most perfect of prayers" (St. Thomas Aquinas), and the "center of the Scriptures" (St. Augustine). The "Our Father" is called "The Lord's Prayer" as it comes from the lips of Jesus himself. It has been integrated into the Divine Office, the sacraments of Christian initiation, and the Eucharistic liturgy itself, so it is truly the prayer of the Church.

There are seven petitions in the "Our Father." The first three point to the Father's glory. The last four point to our needs on the journey towards union with that Father.

"Our Father who art in heaven, hallowed be thy name, thy kingdom come, thy will be done, on earth as it is in heaven. Give us this day our daily bread; and forgive us our trespasses, as we forgive those who trespass against us; and lead us not into temptation, but deliver us from evil."

135

"Our Father." We call God our Father because Jesus, whose brothers and sisters we have become through Baptism, has revealed him to us as Father. Praying to him as Father should both develop the desire to become like him and likewise develop a humble, trusting attitude which leads us to be like little children in the presence of their Father. We call him "our" Father which expresses our conviction that we are indeed his people, that our certain hope is in his ultimate promise, and that we belong to a community of the baptized which together claims him as Father.

"Who art in heaven." Here we are referring not to a place where God is, but rather to a way of being, a way in which God exists. God exists in majesty and is present in the hearts of each of the just.

"Hallowed be thy name." In this petition, we recognize God's name and we acknowledge it as holy. We echo the gradual process of the revelation of that holy name — through Moses and Jesus — and finally to us, and hopefully through us to every person in the world.

"Thy kingdom come." We pray for the final and complete coming of the kingdom in this petition. We pray for that moment when Jesus hands the kingdom over to the Father. We also pray for the coming of the kingdom in our own individual lives at this moment of our existence. This sentiment is summed up in those final words of the Scriptures, "Come, Lord Jesus" (Rv 22:20).

"Thy will be done." The Father has made known his will through his Son, Jesus Christ. In this petition, we acknowledge that will of the Father, and we express our desire to unite our will to that of his Son and our desire to bring about the plan of the Father for our salvation.

The "Our Father," Part II

We now turn to the last four petitions of the "Our Father," petitions which present our needs to the Father.

"Give us this day our daily bread." As a community, aware of our union with one another and our responsibility for one another, we ask the Father to give each of us everything which we need for our daily sustenance, both physical and spiritual. "Daily bread" recalls in a special way the spiritual bread of the Eucharist with which we can nourish ourselves daily. This petition also reminds us of our necessary concern for our brothers and sisters that they, too, receive their daily bread, both material and spiritual.

"And forgive us our trespasses, as we forgive those who trespass against us." As the *Catechism* puts it, "This petition is astonishing" (No. 2838). We ask for forgiveness, boon enough to seek, but we condition that forgiveness of self on the forgiveness which we have extended to others. More, while our petition looks to the future (forgiveness of our sins), our response (forgiveness of others) must come first in time.

"And lead us not into temptation." We beg God not to allow us to enter into temptation. Being put to the trial is different from being tempted. Being tempted is different from consenting to temptation.

We pray that we avoid unnecessary and avoidable temptation in our life and that when tempted we are able, with the help of the grace of the Holy Spirit, to resist.

"But deliver us from evil." The evil which we pray to be delivered from here is not an abstraction but a person, the person of the devil, the father of all lies. We pray that the final victory over the devil, already won by Christ, be shown forth in our lives and our world. We pray to share in this final victory over the devil.

"Amen." Finally, by this last word, the traditional close to Christian prayer, we ratify the prayer which Jesus taught us and make this praise of the Father and these seven petitions our own prayer.